FROM DEATH
DO I PART

FROM DEATH DO I PART

How I Freed Myself From Addiction

Amy Lee Coy

THREE IN THE MORNING PRESS

FROM DEATH DO I PART
How I Freed Myself From Addiction

THREE IN THE MORNING PRESS
P.O. Box 6556
Woodland Hills, California 91365
threeinthemorningpress.com

Printed in the USA
www.printshopcentral.com

Library of Congress Control Number: 2010929371

1. Addiction. 2. Self-Help Techniques 3. Mind and Body
4. Memoirs

ISBN 978-0-692-00971-0

The most beautiful people we have known are those who have known defeat, known suffering, known struggle, known loss, and have found their way out of the depths. These persons have an appreciation, a sensitivity, and an understanding of life that fills them with compassion, gentleness, and a deep loving concern. Beautiful people do not just happen.

Elizabeth Kübler Ross

Contents

Contents

Acknowledgements

My greatest appreciation and love go out to everyone who helped me complete *From Death Do I Part*:

My sister, Adriana, my step-father, Ron, and my husband, John, for the countless hours they spent editing my work and helping me become a better writer. It was the brilliant combination of their expert skills and different writing styles that allowed me to find and express my own writing abilities.

In addition to sharing with me his great professorial writing advice and his musical partnership, my husband also provided me with a most valuable element in my healing process—the psychological space I needed to make the discoveries I have written about in this book. (He also never complained about the sweaty bed sheets night after night that were a result of my severe alcohol withdrawal—in fact, he washed them for me.)

Without the deep love and support from my mother, Susan, this book would not be what it is today. There are some things that many of us hope never to be reminded of, yet, while writing this book, my mother always encouraged me to say whatever I needed to, however painful it might be. In her own life, she has shown the greatest courage, and I thank her with all my heart as I, and so many others, continue to benefit from her incredible bravery, beauty, strength and wisdom.

My father, Larry, and my brother, Matt, also played an important part in the development of this book by supporting me with their love and enthusiasm. It meant a lot to me to have their encouragement.

I give my deepest gratitude and love to all of you, my family. I also want to give my love and appreciation to everyone who struggles with addiction for if you did not exist, I would have believed I was truly alone and would likely never have found my way out of the darkness.

Many thanks to everyone,

Amy

FOREWORD

*A*my Lee Coy is a unique woman. Not unique because she rejected psychiatric medications, rehab, and Alcoholics Anonymous on her way to sobriety after two decades of substance abuse, depression, and alcoholism. Many people perform versions of this "miraculous" self-cure. In fact, a majority of alcoholics and addicts recover for and through themselves, outside of the halls of treatment programs and AA meetings.

She is unique because of her bravery, her clarity of vision, and her ability—and her willingness—to express these things.

Amy Coy always felt alone—partly because her mother left her alone to join a cult. Partly because her grandfather sexually molested her as a child.

Partly because, through hundreds of therapy sessions and AA meetings and rehab groups from the age of 13 on, her own inner lights never turned on. In fact, the psychiatric and rehab facilities she frequently found herself in seemed intent on beating her spirit out of her, and certainly not in giving her room to find her core self.

Finally, at the age of 35, writhing on the floor in a small Pennsylvania town as she withdrew from alcohol and tobacco, she saw her first beacon of light: She would talk to all of those other lonely people, the ones who likewise hadn't been turned on by psychiatry, medications, and the 12 Steps. From this epiphany sprang the germ of *From Death Do I Part*.

And you, lucky reader, are the beneficiary of her fulfillment of this promise to describe her own personal path, the promise that has maintained her sobriety since she first imagined you reading her words. Helping you to help yourself is her goal— just as she finally discovered that only she could help herself. Only then could she let go the despised inner self she has replaced with a generous, creative, comely spirit that matches her radiant outward appearance. A beauty she never before accepted, or believed, she had.

⌘

Amy was always told—like you may have been—that AA and the 12 Steps were the only way for her to recover. That psychiatric meds were the only solution for her depression. But all of these things only made her feel worse about herself. And Amy is not alone in this experience—even AA's biggest fans acknowledge that only a minority (really a quite small minority) stick to and succeed at the "program." Most prescription takers don't find in them a permanent resolution for their mood disorders either. And a distinct minority—like Amy—will attempt suicide while on these meds.

Maybe it was the way professional helpers always seemed to disdain her and to begrudge her the time they were spending talking to her. All they wanted her to do was to cooperate, to be silent, to take the meds they gave her. But Amy wasn't prepared to be obedient—which first got her in trouble when she was kicked out of school at 13. And, she figured, if she were taking prescriptions to modify her true feelings, why not drink? That worked "better" for her, after all.

She was abused in several such institutions as a young teen. After that, she began a modeling career, developed an eating disorder, was married twice—once to an international jet-setting semi-retired lawyer, once to a university professor. And she drank, always drank, to fight off the inner demons, the self-contempt, and the inability to appreciate the world around her.

⌘

Amy doesn't describe herself as being in recovery. She doesn't want to center her identity around her drinking or not drinking—which is one more reason AA meetings aren't for her. For one thing, once she sobered up, she was too busy. Busy writing music, a children's book, and—most important of all—*From Death Do I Part*. She just needed to clear the airwaves to get to these tasks.

> *In my substance-abusing life, I had become bored. Although I was doing most of the basic tasks that life requires, I was uninspired. All that I knew about life depressed me. All that I knew about myself saddened, angered and disappointed me. I was living in a very narrow world, and that reflected upon my opinion of myself. I bottled up all those dismal and dreary feelings of mine, and I used them to define myself. That is how I ended up ugly in my mind.*

Amy discovered:

> *To change that low opinion of myself—to change my alcohol-guzzling, cigarette-smoking identity—it was necessary that I quit ingesting those*

things, of course, but it was also just as important that I allow myself to have new thoughts and opinions about myself as well as about life.

For Amy, the process of overcoming addiction is a process of moving forward—not of labeling herself, not of rehashing her failures and abuse, not of blaming herself or others. She knows—the decades she spent doing these things never allowed her to quit drugs, alcohol, eating problems, cigarettes. Something else did. She needed a new way of thinking about herself and life, one not anchored in the past, or in her trauma, or in the bromides of the 12 Steps or of psychiatry.

It was never satisfying for me to hear, "You are an alcoholic because you have a disease," or, "It's in your genes." For me, such generic explanations of my very personal problems were no help at all. I wanted to understand what was going on with me emotionally in the way I understood what was going on with my body in the yoga class. That way, I would not feel helpless—as I could sense I was not.

I made the choice to quit using alcohol and drugs. In that choice was a commitment to find out how to significantly improve my life—not merely to deny myself the use of substances. Because of that commitment, I needed a deeper understanding of my psychological patterns. So I decided that since it was me who was struggling, then I was my best subject for study. I began to carry out that study by using the powerful tool of self-observation.

⌘

Thus, this book doesn't dwell on Amy Lee Coy's problems. She only describes situations from her past when she wants to illustrate how she has overcome them, and how others might learn to do so. Nor is this a book about religious belief. Nor is it simply a recipe of ways to avoid craving and to sustain sobriety. Rather, it is about the self-discovery that leads to finding satisfaction in life, genuine satisfaction, life-sustaining satisfaction. This discovery includes finding the reasons, and habits, and feelings that underlay the past addictions, so as to sidestep and replace them. It entails modifying thinking, even playing mind games with oneself.

Some call this cognitive behaviorism, or changing thinking, behavior, and the links between them. I call Amy Coy's approach, on the other hand, spiritual behaviorism, a synthesis I have seen performed by no one so well as she. Although our backgrounds and approaches are different, I find the convergence of my ideas with Amy's remarkably reassuring. How could two such different people with two such different exposures to addiction—hers through living and overcoming it, mine through researching, writing about, and treating it—arrive in such similar, compatible places? It seems that we are honing in together on something truthful.

Some might find it strange that I write this foreword for Amy's book, since I have written as a psychologist about addiction for over 30 years. But in all of my books, from *Love and Addiction* to *7 Tools to Beat Addiction*, I emphasize the power of individuals to cure themselves. Of their need to do so.

I have also created a treatment program. But the treatment, called the Life Process Program, is pegged exactly to Amy's life, although I did not know her at the time.

Amy found the occasional urges she had to return to drinking—and smoking—couldn't match the rewards of being herself that she found, and developed, once her life was clear of the miasma of booze and medications. Among her many insights, Amy perceived that, "When I choose immediate gratification, I miss the genuinely gratifying process of working to satisfy the desires of my true nature."

It is exploring these aspects of herself and her experience, past and present, en route to achieving fulfillment, that form Amy's antidote to addiction. Either way—through the Life Process Program, or through processing your own life like Amy did—you will travel a similar road to escape addiction. Or better yet, you will find the same path into yourself to accept the person you are and that you can be. Not the same person as Amy Lee Coy. She's taken. Her words will help you to find yourself.

There are several overarching things on which Amy and I agree. One is the importance of having a purpose in life: "Feeling that we have a purpose in life, a positive reason to be healthier and to make changes, makes a huge difference when it comes to quitting an addictive habit."

As for regrets for the lost years, "I can now see that there are still many, many positive—and joyful—things that I can do for myself and for others in every moment that I am alive."

And one last crucial thing we share is the value, the power, of the self, of yourself:

Although I believed that I was doomed to end up sick, drunk and miserable, I was not. It is never too late to revive your spirit and to care for your body. No matter how deep you think you have sunk into the misery of addiction, all is never lost. You always have the option to discover your strength and change the choices that you make.

You can lift yourself into a new, healthier life.

Which is why Amy wrote this hopeful, inspiring, encouraging book, beginning it as she did in her deepest depths of despair and aloneness.

STANTON PEELE, PH.D., J.D.
Author, *Love and Addiction:*
7 Tools to Beat Addiction
Founder, Life Process Program,
May 15, 2010

Chapter 1

Toxic

"Barns burnt down,
Now I can see the moon."

Mizuta Masahide

I found myself crouched on the living room floor, shaking, sweating, and in shock. My heart was pounding so hard that I felt as if I had two hearts—one thumping viciously in my head. I was cold and clammy, and then I was soaking wet with sweat. Freezing and sweating, hot and cold, trembling and shivering—for hours and hours. But the worst part of all was the horrible *fear*.

Here I was, thirty-five years old and still battling the same self-inflicted sickness of addiction that I had desperately fought with since I was a young teenager.

I had been through detox many times before,

even as recently as two months before this, but I had never felt terror consume me the way it was now. I had experienced the sweats before. Beginning in my early twenties, whenever I stopped drinking for a few days, I would get terrible night sweats, and if I managed to sleep at all, I would wake up sopping wet.

Back then I didn't really care that much. I just figured that my body was cleansing and flushing out toxins. I did not feel any psychological disturbances other than the obvious and extremely intense desire for a drink and a smoke.

I almost always quit smoking when I managed to temporarily quit drinking. It seemed logical to me that way. Quitting both at the same time helped me think I was serious about making changes and getting healthy. The few times I quit drinking but kept smoking, it was too easy for me to give in to a drink since I was clearly not fully committed to my greatest health. And besides that, smoking and drinking literally went hand in hand for me—what good was one without the other.

But something was different this time. The physical and mental horror—lying on the floor, screaming inside with terror and confusion—was a new depth of alcohol devastation for me. It was the most horrifying dread I had ever experienced from alcohol. I was stunned. And to make my fears even worse, it seemed that I had nowhere to turn. I felt helpless, terrified and alone.

I grew up in Southern California, in and around Los Angeles, and I always managed to find someone in that big city that I could turn to— someone who had experience with alcohol withdrawal, or at least someone who knew me and my "stuff." Even if I didn't buy into their theories, there was at least someone I could talk to who understood the withdrawal experience.

Here, living far away from home in a small town in Pennsylvania, feeling more terror than I thought possible, and experiencing severe physical withdrawals, accompanied by overwhelming internal chaos and panic, I was lost. Although I had been in Pennsylvania for almost four years, I had yet to "live" there. In fact, I hated it there. It felt so unfamiliar and oppressive that, at times, I actually had a physical sensation of choking. I felt trapped, with no escape. I spent most of my time in my house alone. I had no friends, and I didn't have a doctor I could trust. I could talk with my husband, who was the reason why I was living in Pennsylvania in the first place, but he had no firsthand experience working with people with addictions. I felt I needed someone who knew *exactly* what I was going through.

I had spent hours on the phone and on the Internet, trying to find someone to help me locally. Nothing. I even went to a "New Agey" sort of counselor in town. She was very nice but insisted that I attend AA, Alcoholics Anonymous. She thought that was essential and told me there was no way around that fact.

I knew all too well the ways of AA—daily meetings, sponsors, the 12 Steps, thirty-day rehabs and the countless hours of tales of drunkenness I had heard so many times before. I had been through all of that so many times from the age of thirteen that I just could not bear it again. But that, and a bit of yoga, was all that she had to offer me. So I thanked her and never went back.

When therapists and doctors don't know what to do, they always seem to defer to AA. I personally do not like AA. I don't like the way it makes me feel. I always felt worse about myself, my life, and my future while attending the meetings. Of course, if AA works for someone, then they should certainly use it. I know it's great for some people, but I have always had trouble with it. And yes, I have worked the Steps completely—more than once. And yes, I have had a sponsor—more than one. And yes, I have tried it as an adult—as well as at age thirteen, fifteen, seventeen, twenty-six, twenty-eight, and thirty. I have done my time with AA.

Yet that day, crawling on the floor in my own sweat, I felt so desperate that I actually considered going to the only AA meeting in town. I felt that helpless. But I also felt sure that AA would not be any different than it ever was. Even though I was terrified, in withdrawal, and feeling helpless and alone, I just could not bring myself to go to a meeting. I needed more than that.

It was then that I realized that if I was going to get help, it was going to have to come from me and nowhere else. So now, not only was I suffering from the complete panic and nausea of a massive detox experience, and not only did I have to be the one to calm and comfort myself, but I had to be a superhero as well and rescue myself. I was angry. I was scared. I was sick. And I was extremely worried about what I could do next.

But I had made up my mind to do something to help myself. I was sweating and trembling and horrified, yet I became 100 percent determined that I had to do this. I was sick of all of the promises. I needed help, and I knew that others like me did as well.

Thinking about all the time that I had already spent listening to the so-called authorities on addiction, I felt anger. I had put a lot of trust in those people and spent a lot of money on them, and still I was sick. I didn't want to be sick. But even if I had a million dollars to spend on my recovery, I couldn't think of a single place to spend that money where I felt I would truly be helped.

What became clear to me at that moment was that I had lived my life of addictions on a very lonely path, and now, unless I was willing to accept defeat, I had to accept, at least for a while, that I would recover on a lonely path as well.

When I speak of being on the lonely path, I am not talking about simply being alone; I am describing the deep inner feelings of isolation that some of us experience. When I felt this deep inner aloneness, there was very little that anyone could *say* to me to stop me from having this baffling and distressing inner experience of absolute separation. It's a feeling that cannot be easily penetrated. I had made such a shell out of my feelings of sadness, depression and despair that it was difficult for me to experience the warmth and caring of others.

That is why I could not work with groups like AA which, at their best, offered companionship and a group experience. To those who benefit from such togetherness, lucky them—truly. But for me, where others would feel supported and delighted that they were no longer alone, I would feel more alone than ever. The caring of the group seemed to be acts of duty; the practices superficial; and the Steps, of course, repetitive and dull. I was, without doubt, on what I call *the lonely path of addiction.*

So, in the middle of the worst detox I had ever experienced, I realized that if I wanted to rise above my struggles, I was going to have to figure this out for myself. I vowed that if I discovered any way out or learned anything at all, I would share it with others that suffer as I was suffering then. I resolved right there to hold on to see what—if anything—is at the end of the rainbow...on the other side of the fence...across the bridge....

On that day, in that moment, on that floor, bathed in sweat and tears of despair, this book began. This is the book I wanted in my moments of terror, desperation, and defeat. When I first quit drinking—and all the other habits that went along with my drinking—writing this book got me through the worst of those times. By offering me the hope of a possible solution for my struggles, this book inspired me to go on.

And now that I can breathe again, I give this

book to you. I hope that it will help get you through similar kinds of the extremely difficult and seemingly impossible moments I encountered as I sobered up. I hope my story will inspire you—or at least give you something to hold on to until you get over a few of the humps. I want you to understand that even when you are on the lonely path of addiction, you are not completely alone in your aloneness, or even in your misery. I know how bad—how really bad—it feels, but I also know that if you can hang on a little longer, that feeling of badness can lighten and even fade away.

If nothing else, at least now you know there is someone out there who understands, someone who has been on the same devastating path. And I can help guide you if you want to recover. I know how nervous, miserable, and wasted you feel because I have felt all of that myself—for a very long time, in a very deep way. Yet I am also someone who, finally, after so many attempts and so many failures, has learned to accept, appreciate and enjoy more of life without using alcohol or drugs. And now I am able to share my discoveries with you.

⌘

Chapter 2

ℋELP

"Conventional opinion is the ruin of our souls."

Rumi

*B*y day two of my miserable detox ordeal, I could not handle the hallucinations. Although my nerves were so shot that I had practically become agoraphobic, I was able to walk to the doctor down the block—small town.

He called my symptoms "waking nightmares." You can say that again. I had heard about this in my early twenties from my ex-husband, who had noticed my night sweats on the few occasions when I didn't drink. He was a semi-retired defense attorney and apparently knew something about it—from his clients or his colleagues, I never knew. He called the hallucinations "delirium tremens" (DT's). Although I listened, I put the information aside. I was sure I would never let myself go that far.

Oh, how ten years can fly by—especially when you're wasted.

So there I was, in the small-town doctor's office, exposing my badness. I was bad, bad, bad. I was sure they wanted me out of their town even more than I wanted to go. I was tainting their neighborhood with my sickly behavior. Bad, bad, bad, bad was what I felt. I wanted to hide, but I desperately needed some help.

However fearful I was of being condemned by everyone in the doctor's office and whatever rumors about me I feared might fly around town, I was far more afraid of the worsening nightmares, hallucinations, and frightening, sweat-filled, sleepless nights. I needed help. I needed something to stop the horrifying mental visions I was having.

The doctor had to reassure me that I was not going to die and that I was only having withdrawals. Only. Only! My heart seemed to be pounding throughout my body. Sometimes it was all I could hear. I was sure I had pushed my body too far this time. I kept asking him to check my heart, and he eventually did listen to it. I suspect he did that more to calm me down than for his information.

The doctor also talked to me somberly about getting help. I knew that I needed something, but his generic suggestions of AA, therapy, and possibly a psychiatrist for medication were not very hopeful or helpful to me. But I was broken and desperate and seemingly without options, so I listened to him without resistance. I was so desperate for help that I did not even tell him about the many rehabs I had been in before, the hundreds and hundreds of AA meetings I had attended throughout my life, and the many different medications I had taken in the past. I would only have wasted what little energy I had left in my body. It would have been of no interest to him anyway. He had nothing else to say.

So I gratefully took the calming medication he gave me that afternoon, and I took it again that night. Thankfully, that allowed me a somewhat more restful evening. The night was still terrible, but switching from "horrifying" to "really bad" was an improvement. However, I guess I needed an even higher dose of the medication than the doctor had prescribed because I continued to have cold sweats all night. But the sweats alone were not as frightening to me as the hallucinations had been, so I just accepted the situation. Although the nightmares stopped right away with the medication, it took about five days for the sweats to end.

Still tormented and still within days of having quit drinking, limited by what my insurance would pay for and by the lack of available options, I found myself a few days later sitting in the very desolate waiting room of a local mental health clinic. As this was not my first visit to such a place, I was able to recognize its "type" right away: It was a financial clinic—cold and stiff. I did not see this as a place of integrity or a place with a passion for helping and healing. I was in the waiting room of a system that does not seem to be very good at helping people in my extreme predicament. However, it does seem to be very good at collecting fees.

Behind the glass window looking into the reception area, I noticed several women going on about their business, occasionally peering over at me as if I were some kind of frog in biology class. Finally, after a pointlessly long wait, they opened the window, took my forms, and then abruptly closed the window on me. I took a deep breath. I knew this game all too well. I was desperate and I was tired, but I was not stupid.

Later, after being escorted down the cold

hospital-like corridor by a young, oddly cheerful female student-in-training from the local college, I was seated and questioned. I felt as if I was helping her rather than the other way around, and I really had to bite my tongue to hang in there and not snap back at her or run out the door.

After she was through and left the room, I was greeted by a therapist-in-training. I was definitely a frog in biology class. However, I was patient and sat through the fifty-minute session, answering whatever particulars the "therapist" asked me for. I also proceeded to ask a few questions of my own, and based on my experience in the place up to that point, I was not surprised to find there had been no changes in the world of psychotherapy or dealing with addictions during my four-year absence.

That useless interview was the only thing they had to offer me in my time of crisis, so I left feeling discouraged and even *more* troubled than before. But as miserable as I felt, it was a significant moment for me. It was the first time that this book—at the time it was only the idea for this book—saved me. Thinking about writing a book that could help people who were in a situation like mine motivated me because I knew that we needed better care and support than was currently available. I knew that I had to keep going. I wanted to jump out a window, but I had made a decision and a promise to discover better solutions for people who were struggling as I was then. I was determined to find out if there was something better than drinking and, more importantly, something much better than the mundane, robotic sobriety that I had known in my previous short-lived attempts at it. I did not want to give up alcohol for just another version of misery.

In that moment I felt very, very alone. I did not feel as if I had a single ally. I was a lone rebel on a lonely path. But this rebel was going to do this thing, no matter what. And so, with that determination to keep me going, I went home and got back in bed.

⌘

Chapter 3

ALONE

"There are many here among us,
who feel that life is but a joke."

All Along the Watchtower
Bob Dylan

*I*n spite of my disappointment with the last treatment center, I persevered in looking for help. I was still very sick, and I really could have used a friend—or anyone, really—who understood my struggles. However, I still could not find a single person to relate to. The few people I did find who were willing to discuss my problem with me—and these were people in help centers I found online—only directed me to AA or psychotherapy or antidepressant medication as my solution. I can't blame them because, at that time, those were the only choices I knew about as well.

But I was determined. There had to be *more*. There had to be more because I was not better yet.

I continued to reach out by searching the Internet and making phone calls, and the more I did that, the more I found myself needing to reach *in*—to myself—for comfort. When I expressed discouragement with psychotherapy and the other offered options, I was told again and again that I was "in denial." I could see that this was not going to be easy.

It was not until months later, after I had struggled through early sobriety on my own, that I was able to locate people who supported other ways of quitting addictive habits, and those only partially appealed to me. However, those people were not local to me, so I could not participate or even investigate whether they might be able to help me. I was isolated and struggling, and I was not sure how to help myself, but I was sure there had to be a way.

At this point I was more willing to accept help than I had ever been throughout my addicted life. I was broken down, and I really wanted to be guided, nurtured, and helped. But no matter how I tried or where I looked, it seemed as though no one had the type of guidance I was seeking. My heart and my mind were willing, but I was unable to find anyone who was able to help me. That was not just because I was in a small town. When I was growing up in Los Angeles, I had also been unable to find anything that helped me get well. But at least in Los Angeles there was always some sort of support group or personal growth type of event going on I could go to. This time, however, I was finding nothing.

Although throughout my life I had family and friends and more than my share of lovers, as far as my addictive habits were concerned, I always felt I was alone. I felt different, even among other people who drank heavily and smoked constantly. Some of my therapists had accused me of being stubborn and hard to reach. Of course, I always refused to believe that was the problem. Now, however, I was feeling such a desperate need for assistance that I began to think they might have been right—maybe my stubborn personality was the problem.

As it turned out, that stubborn personality trait is a large part of what saved my life. My strong determination to find some way to truly help myself was my stubbornness working *for* me. But in spite of my understanding of that, the lack of validation during my early days of recovery made it difficult for me to keep my determination strong.

I did not feel I was in denial by refusing to attend AA. I was extremely aware of how unhealthy and even dangerous my substance-abusing behaviors had become. But I was also aware that every time I gave up drinking and smoking, I became even more miserable. That was my problem. Why in the world would I want to trade the moderately tolerable misery and depression that I had with drinking and smoking for intense agony and even deeper despair when I gave up those things? That is what I resolved, once and for all, to find out.

As I went along day by day, weighing my choice—to drink or not to drink—I found it helpful knowing that there might be a purpose to this terrible struggle I was in. In fact, I not only found it helpful, I found it invaluable for my sobriety. The purpose was that someday I might be able to offer a ray of hope to another struggling person in similar turmoil to myself.

It's something to think about. There are millions of people in terrible sadness and despair, and when you are able to finally catch your own breath and regain your inner strength and balance, someone in those millions could really use your support.

There were many times during my early recovery when I came to my computer to write and I didn't even know what I was going to say. I just knew I needed to do something active. Even though I would sit down feeling horrible, angry, or frustrated, once I was able to connect with a core desire to help others, I began to relax. By the time I finished writing, I felt surer of myself—calmer, stronger, and even slightly successful.

So in the very beginning of my struggle, as all my attempts to find outside support failed, I made a decision. I decided that if I could not find an ally for myself, then the least I could do was become an ally for someone else. So the idea of helping others kept me going, even when I didn't feel I had anything to share but a flat-out desire for a drink.

At that stage, in the beginning of my recovery, writing became extremely helpful to me. It didn't matter that my formal education pretty much ended when I was fourteen years old, when I was expelled from the Los Angeles public school system for excessive truancy, poor grades, and foul language. It didn't matter that my fingers were poking at the keys rather than eloquently and effortlessly flying over them. It mattered that I did it at all. That mattered.

If you find yourself with a lack of available help and a lack of understanding, you might want to try writing or some other form of self-expression with the motivation that someday you might be able to uplift someone else who suffers as you have—someone who also needs to know that they are not alone in the despair that they feel. Aiming to help others can be a great way to sustain your strength, your will, your desire for more joy and therefore your new, healthier life-style. As I found out during my dark days of recovery, something encouraging happens when you intend to help others.

⌘

Chapter 4

TROUBLE

*"The image is one thing and
the human being is another.
It is very hard to live up to the image."*

Elvis

In order to demonstrate to you the potential of your own healing, I want to briefly tell you a little about my life and some of my past experiences. There was a drastic contrast between what people saw on the outside and the reality of what was happening on the inside. I believe that is true for many of us who suffer with addictions, and I hope that by sharing with you the depth of despair from which I have healed, you can believe it is possible for you to overcome your struggles as well.

Santa Barbara, California, where I was born, is one of the more sought after, glamorous coastal cities in Southern California. It has gorgeous beaches, where I played as a child, and a spectacular mountain range, where my dad would take me and my older brother and sister camping and fishing. I also have fond memories of walking playfully along the train tracks and eating wild berries. There were many fun things for children to do in such a beautiful place.

When I was in the third grade, I was classified as a "mentally gifted minor" (or M.G.M. child) by the Board of Education. According to the tests that I had been given, this was supposed to mean that I had an unusually high IQ and that I was "special," gifted.

When I was sixteen, I got a modeling contract with the Nina Blanchard Modeling Agency in Hollywood. It was one of the best and most prestigious agencies of its kind at that time.

When I was twenty-three, I met a wealthy older man, and within weeks I moved into his beachfront home in Malibu. He owned several other homes around the world, and shortly after I moved in, we were traveling around the world together. Within two years we were married at the legendary Hotel Bel-Air in Los Angeles—swans and all.

During that marriage I spent a great deal of

time traveling around Greece, England, Hawaii, the islands of the West Indian Ocean, and other exotic locations on various overseas adventures. For several years I sported a great tan and an exciting passport.

This all might sound quite wonderful, but let me tell you this same story again from the point of view of how I actually experienced it. I will share with you some of my more private details in order to help you feel—in spite of possibly an entire lifetime of misery—that there is still hope for peace and happiness in your life.

My parents were divorced when I was five years old. I stayed in Santa Barbara with my father and my older brother and sister while my mother moved into a large house with some of her friends, all of whom were strangers to me. One year later, she moved to Los Angeles to join the spiritual cult that she had been involved with for some time before the divorce.

Given the extraordinarily difficult circumstances of her own childhood, I can understand and empathize with my mother's choices of that time. However, as a very young child and for many years thereafter, I assumed and believed that she simply loved the cult people more than she loved me. I deeply loved my mother, and the thought that she did not love me in the same way torment-ed and troubled me throughout my childhood. Ironically, her absence became a dominating presence in my life. Losing my mother was devas-tating for me, and I did not handle it well. I cried a lot, I had a terrible time sleeping, and I wet my bed often.

Approximately a year after being identified as an M.G.M. student, my grades had fallen and were no longer those of a gifted child. During the worst period of this time, at the age of eleven, I became suicidal. I often thought about death as I held a sharp knife or a bottle of pills to my stom-ach. I wondered if death might be better than the constant sadness, panic, and heartache that I struggled with daily.

In addition to suffering the devastating loss of my mother, I was also enduring the perverse actions of my grandfather. As I remember, he began molesting me right after my mother left us. He would read me stories from Doctor Seuss while reaching his hand into my underwear. Of course I liked the stories, but I found the touching very bizarre, extremely uncomfortable, and abso-lutely confusing. My grandmother would often be just around the corner in another room, but she never came in. It was an odd and frightening experience for me as a young girl.

When I was eleven and my parents eventually saw that the family could no longer continue on with me in such constant turmoil, I was permitted to move to Los Angeles to live with my mother. At the time I felt that this was a tremendous, lifesaving move for me. I was ecstatic—but only for a short while.

Soon after moving to my mother's house in L.A., my previous feelings of fear and despair—not to mention the turmoil of puberty—began to creep into my life. It was at that time that I began drinking, drugging, and having sex with—well, it didn't really matter. I would sleep with whoever had the drink or the drug.

All of this self-destructive behavior landed me in many drug and alcohol rehabilitation clinics, beginning at age 13 and ending at age 31. However, my self-destructive behavior did not come to an end until I was 35, when I found myself curled up on my living room floor, bathed in sweat and fear as I suffered through my worst detox experience ever. It was then that I was forced to make the simple choice—to live or to die. My body was in crisis and on a rapid decline towards death.

In addition to all of the drinking, smoking and sexing that I did over the years, I had also developed an eating disorder when I was thirteen years old. I did not know what to call it at the time, but I was both bulimic and anorexic. So, in addition to the damaging effects of all the substances that I had been using, I was also severely malnourished. I had been starving my body on and off for many years, and I had to be hospitalized several times because of it.

When I married my first husband—the wealthy one who lived on the beach in Malibu—I was still drinking several bottles of wine every day as well as vodka and beer. Though I may have been financially free, I was by no means happy. In fact, all the pristine and luscious paradises that we visited were lost on me. In a few of those gorgeous locales, my husband owned homes. We had an amazing home overlooking the Mediterranean Sea on Santorini Island in Greece. At sunset I would often perch myself on a nearby wall with wine and cigarette in hand and gaze out at the paradisiacal ocean, only to feel intense sadness and despair.

Eventually, while in a fancy Malibu drug and alcohol rehab, I began divorce proceedings—suggested and encouraged by the in-house therapist I had been seeing for less than a week. After the divorce I struggled for money, and I continued to struggle for my emotional well-being. I had several more hospital/treatment stays, and I kept up my self-destructive behaviors until that horrible day in Pennsylvania when, on my knees, I vowed to help myself—myself.

But because I was able to keep my struggles so well hidden, it was possible to look at me and think that I had an idyllic life. Unfortunately, appearance is all that it was for me. In reality, I was so distraught and so numb to feeling the ordinary joys of life, I was unable to be emotionally moved by even the most spectacular sights that I was so privileged to see. I had the intellectual knowledge about all of the beautiful places, and I certainly understood that I was supposed to be enamored by it all, but I was suffering so intensely with my torturous emotions that it became impossible for me to *feel* the joys of the amazing beauty that surrounded me daily.

However, even while I was suffering, I recognized that to others my life appeared to be a dream come true. For that reason, when I tried to share how I was truly feeling, I often sensed people perceiving me as spoiled and ungrateful. It was much easier for me to let people believe that I was the happy girl on the beach or the beautiful model in the pictures. I was sure that no one would understand the deeply tormented and distraught person that I really was.

So, while the *appearance* was that I was living a dream life of privilege, the *reality* in my private world was that I was feeling heartache, depression, and despair, accompanied by periodic suicidal feelings. I was also engaging daily in addictive behaviors that were killing me.

⌘

Chapter 5

CAGED

*"I got a simple rule about everybody.
If you don't treat me right, shame on you!"*

Louis Armstrong

When I was thirteen I had become such a burden and worry to my family that I was sent off to my first drug and alcohol rehab. In 1984 rehabs were not in the media as they are today, and in fact, it was rare that you would meet or hear of someone who had stayed in one. So for me at the time it was terrifying to be there and I had no idea what to expect.

The facility was a dreary institution that had once been a hospital. The hospital-style beds and bathrooms, the barren floors, the cardboard ceilings, the dingy walls—all remained intact, except that most of the beds were now broken and security locks had been added to most of the doors so that the patients could not escape.

One day on the adolescent unit, my new temporary home, my fellow patients and I had a riot. It was set off by an exasperated patient, but he was quickly joined and encouraged by me and most of the other kids on the unit. We all shared his frustration and outrage about being locked up and unable to freely do as we pleased.

We went wild that day. Someone managed to set off the overhead sprinkler system, and in the chaos one of the male patients was able to climb out through the roof, run to a nearby liquor store, and come back with a pint of whisky. Even though that was not nearly enough to satisfy all fifteen of us, it added a great deal to the drama as everyone got even more excited.

Someone busted open the locked doors that led out to the "yard." Even though it was mainly asphalt, it was nice to be free. We tried to ignore the fact that there was still a fence around the yard to keep us in. We were all screaming and yelling, and I think a few of the patients actually escaped the premises.

Inside the building, everyone on the staff was understandably shaken by our little riot. But what happened next was just wrong.

I had become particularly close to one of the patients. He was quite large and overweight, but unusually kind and gentle. In the chaos he got extremely loud, as many of us did. The staff evidently perceived him as threatening. However, instead of locking him up in his room or in another room somewhere else on the premises to cool down, the staff ordered needles and shot him up with a tranquilizer. After he was knocked unconscious, they shipped him off by ambulance to a psychiatric hospital for a seventy-two hour hold.

After they took my friend away, the staff sent off another patient to the same hospital. As I saw that happening, I became frightened that I would be next, especially since I was one of the more vocal ones in the commotion. Luckily, since I was under age, they needed parental consent in order to do that.

The first chance I got, I called my mother on the patient payphone and begged her to promise me that she would not give them permission to take me away. She gave me her promise.

Sadly, in spite of that promise, within hours I found myself waiting for my own ambulance ride to the psychiatric hospital. Not only was I terribly afraid of this foreboding destination—a "loony" hospital—but I was deeply hurt that my mother had broken her promise to me.

I now know that someone at the hospital had called my mother, had frightened her about my condition, and coerced her into changing her mind. But at the time I just thought she had broken her word and betrayed me. Clearly, the rehab staff people in charge of making that monumental decision to send an adolescent off to a psych ward did not understand, or *care*, how important trust is with a loved one, especially between parent and child. So the people in charge of me, the ones in charge of "curing" me, carelessly undermined the trust between me and my mother.

When the ambulance arrived, they tried to carry me out on a stretcher, which I refused. I was not happy about the situation, and I insisted that I walk. After I had climbed into the ambulance, the EMTs (Emergency Medical Technicians) were not very friendly. They refused to communicate with me at all throughout the whole ride to the hospital.

It was a very strange ride in that ambulance. I was acting tough, but I was actually extremely frightened. I was not hyper or out of control, and their refusal to speak to me only deepened my fear of where they were taking me.

By this time it was dark, and after leaving the

city of Inglewood, I had no idea where we were or where I was going. Refusing to lay on the gurney, I sat up and quietly stared out the window at the night and the city lights for the entire eerie ride. I was thirteen years old and feeling such a deep sense of despair and disappointment that it even rivaled my suicidal emotions of the years before.

I had gone AWOL from this rehab before. A man on the staff, a maintenance man, unbolted my window and snuck me and another female patient out in the middle of the night. He and a friend he had brought along got us drunk and nearly succeeded in raping both of us. After a long night of strong resistance, we were somehow able to convince the men to let us go. In a daze we found our way back to the rehab. When we got back, we were punished for escaping. They had a "level" system, and we were both dropped to the very bottom level, which meant no visitors, no weekend passes, and worst of all, no freedom to walk out to the lobby where we would buy our cigarettes and candy.

Now, as I was being rushed through the dark night to the psychiatric hospital for more treatment, I wondered why the people in this rehab suddenly cared so much about my well-being.

As we arrived at the hospital and as I was

escorted through several solid heavy security doors, my insides froze. Looking ahead, I saw the blank faces of the patients as they wandered the halls or leaned against the wall. They looked so weary and vacant that I could not tell whether I was on an adolescent unit or an adult unit. A huge knot of fear grew in my stomach.

The worst part of this experience was the stubborn silence of the people in charge. No one would tell me anything.

I quickly came to understand that asking questions was as dangerous as being quiet. I began to notice that while they *pretended* not to see me, they were actually very closely observing every-thing I did. This was extremely frightening to me because I felt that whether I talked or remained silent, either way I would be risking a serious diagnosis that might keep me imprisoned for a very long time.

I was trapped.

They put me in a bare white room with no windows. They made me give up all my belong-ings, my rings and my other jewelry, and then left me there alone.

I had absolutely no idea what to expect. I thought that they might give me a shot like they had given my friends. Maybe they would give me an electric shock, or even a lobotomy like in the movies. I had no idea. I was at their mercy, and I was really scared.

I was alone in that room for a long time. Eventually, a not-so-friendly woman came in and asked me some questions. Then she took me to a room that had nothing in it but two beds and an obviously drugged-up roommate lying in one of the beds.

At one point I was just sitting on my bed when two people came in, a nurse and another woman. The nurse grabbed my left arm and jabbed a needle into it.

I was petrified. The needle made a puff of air under my skin. I had had my blood drawn constantly at the drug rehab, sometimes even being rudely awakened in the early morning hours to be stabbed by their needle. I was, to some extent, used to that. But this was new. I had no idea what they were doing to me now.

Later, I found out that it had something to do with testing for Tuberculosis. The point is that they didn't tell me anything, and I was so terrified of saying anything that might give them a reason to keep me longer that I couldn't even ask why they were sticking that needle in my arm.

When it was time to eat, they took me down

the hall to another barren but larger cafeteria-type room. I didn't know what to do there either. They make a note of everything that you do in a place like that. I didn't know if crazy people were known to drink chocolate milk or regular milk. Would I appear less crazy if I had yogurt instead…or is *that* abnormal behavior? I wasn't hungry anyway, but if I didn't eat, wouldn't that be some sort of sign of something too? I didn't know what to do. I was very, very alone. Looking back, I cannot believe that anyone, especially the so-called "helpers," would traumatize a child like that and not understand that they were adding to the problem.

When they sat me in front of the chief psychiatrist on the unit for my required evaluation, I anxiously looked around his cold little office and tried to explain to him what had happened—that the riot was just a bunch of locked-up teenagers letting off steam. I tried to explain why I was there, that I had just gotten overly excited, and that I wasn't crazy.

How mistaken I was to think that he cared. I don't think the man even blinked the whole time I was in there. He sat there sternly staring and scowling at me from behind an unimpressive barrier that *looked* like a standard cheap metal desk but was obviously used as a tool to separate the doctor from the patient. He had nothing to say to me. He was the perfect personification of all the psychiatric and psychological professionals that I have encountered in my many "therapeutic" treatments. He appeared to me to be wholly insincere and self-concerned. This particular doctor happened to be extremely cold and condescending, to add to his charm.

What confusion such people must have to believe that they are being of service. I have heard that there are sincere and genuinely altruistic psychiatric professionals operating in these sorts of institutions and rehabilitation centers, but in my experiences, that was not true.

Finally, a day later, I was allowed a phone call to my mom. The phone was right at the nurse's station so they could hear everything that I said. I was afraid that if they heard me beg to get out of there then they might throw away the key forever. Who knows how that might be interpreted. I had to be very careful about what I said.

Doing my best to speak in code, I got the message across to my mother that this place was *not* for me. I tried to explain how terrifying and unpredictable this place was, but since my mom had already agreed to let them take me away back at the first rehab, it was not so easy for her to get me back after that. When my parents were finally able to do so, it was only to return me to the very rehab that had sent me to the psych hospital in the first place.

Later on, I discovered the *real* reason for the psychiatric/rehab facility patient exchange. It was not at all for our benefit or even for the safety of anyone near us. It turns out that the rehab facility received a huge *re-admittance fee* for each one of us that they sent away, discharged, and then re-admitted. They got somewhere in the range of ten thousand dollars for each re-admission they processed.

That is when I first began to suspect that the motives of people in treatment centers are not always to help the patients, but that they are willing to make some of their therapeutic decisions on the basis of how much money it will bring into their organization and their own pockets. In my case I consider what happened to me and to the others patients they sent off to that psych ward psychologically abusive. What an irony that such abuse came at the hands of people who had taken the Hippocratic Oath in which they vowed, "Above all, do no harm."

⌘

Chapter 6

MEDICINE

"We fought him hard, we fought him well,
Out on the plains we gave him hell.
But many came, too much for Cree,
Oh will we ever be set free?"

Run To The Hills
Iron Maiden

*T*he last time I was in a rehab-type facility, I was 31 years old, and I was being treated for depression. It was quite a bizarre experience. They had me on so much medication that at times I lost consciousness. My father told me later that we had a very long conversation, of which I remember nothing. Looking back, it is extremely disturbing to me that an institution of healing would keep me so drugged when I was supposed to be working to heal my emotions.

Forgetting a conversation was not a strange or even a rare occurrence when I was drinking. But when I was not drinking, as in this particular mental "health" facility, it was a definite cause for alarm. I was under the 24-hour supervision and care of several doctors. That care included being on heavy doses of several different mood stabilizers and antidepressants.

The several weeks I was there are all confusion and blanks to me, but I do remember passing out twice and falling to the floor. I happen to remember that because the physical pain of both falls shocked me into some sort of consciousness. The first time, I was doing something in my room, and I was so drugged up that I fell and injured my knee. The second time, I had just finished talking to one of the psychiatrists, and I passed out while getting up to leave. I hurt my ankle pretty badly, and it shocked me awake. I remember that the doctor did not seem at all concerned. In fact, he seemed to care more about the polish on his shoes that he was staring at more than anything that was going on with me at the time. However, I was hurt badly enough that he finally called for an x-ray machine to be brought to the little room that we were in.

Up until that point I thought I was in a

hospital. But bringing in the X-ray machine was such an ordeal for them that it became clear to me that it was not a true hospital.

What struck me through all of the procedure for my ankle was how *disinterested* the doctors and the staff seemed to be. Once they determined that I had not broken any bones, the doctor disappeared, the technicians left, and *no adjustments were made to the medication that they were giving me.* I'm not sure what those doctors thought they were doing. I had been blacking out just fine on my own with the alcohol and my own drugs. I did not need their medications to help me pass out!

I came out of that place the same way that I went in—despairing over my life. I was no better when I came home, even though I had followed their orders and had taken all of their drugs for weeks. I was in such a deep, medication-induced fog the entire time I was there that I could not possibly have accomplished anything significant or worthwhile toward my healing. When I left that place, the only thing different about me was the slight limp from my ankle injury.

Throughout all of this and for the greater part of my life up to that point, all of the supposed healers who were licensed to prescribe medication did so, and most every one of those who weren't, encouraged me to take it. They were always pushing some sort of antidepressants or anti-stress or anti-something my way.

Today this approach of popping a pill to treat emotional difficulties is very common for children of fifteen, thirteen, twelve, or even younger in age. But in 1985, when I was fifteen and I was prescribed my first antidepressant medication, taking drugs for feeling miserable was not so ordinary. As I have learned more about the drug industry and their hugely increased profits, I can see that I was a guinea pig then for what has now become common practice and big business.

They gave me a drug called *Amitriptyline*. This was shortly before Prozac became all the rage. But sadly, Prozac and many other similar types of drugs eventually made their way down my throat too. What a nightmare.

I have a very low opinion of the psychiatrists who gave me so many drugs, as well as the psychologists who supported them. I do, however, appreciate the counselors I have known who supported my desire not to take medication as an option. In my various therapy sessions throughout the years, I have found counselors to be the closest thing to "real" people. They seem to be the most able to show genuine concern and believable compassion. Surely plenty of people have met with truly concerned, caring, and compassionate psychiatrists or psychotherapists. I, however, was never so fortunate.

I do not think I am exaggerating my numbers when I say that in my more than 25 years of treatment, I have seen hundreds of therapy-type persons with all levels of training. Of all of those people, I have only found comfort, understanding, and small snippets of hope with the lesser-schooled. Perhaps for some who have serious psychiatric/medical conditions or those deemed dangerous to themselves or others, a psychiatrist and medication are in order, but for me and the people like me that I have known in the rehabs and hospitals, this "drug first" approach did absolutely nothing to *heal* our difficulties.

Even though in my struggles through the years, I was depressed and did not want to be depressed, I never liked antidepressant drugs. The assumption that there was something wrong with how my brain worked and that drugs were needed to correct it was unsettling, to say the least. I felt (and still do) that there was nothing defective in the functioning of my brain. My difficulties were related to my *emotional* health—my painful feelings, fears, and overall emotional confusion.

I know all too well the theory that long-term emotional strain alters brain chemistry. Many of my doctors preached this theory to me, and they used it to convince me to buy and take the various medications. However, I believe that if this theory were true—that my emotions could alter my brain chemistry for the worst—then it would also be true that my emotions and inner experiences could be just as capable of altering my brain chemicals right back to where they belong. Either way, I was not able to achieve success with any of the drugs, so I continued to search for other ways to live. One of the ways was alcohol.

Although alcohol is classified as a depressant, it often felt like an *antidepressant* to me. At times I could practically feel my neurotransmitters dancing for joy just thinking about having a drink and a smoke.

Also, when life was tough, as it almost always *seemed* to be for me, I did my own "over-prescribing" and misusing of drugs. The difference between that self-medicating and the prescribing of psychiatric drugs is that I always knew it was not a solution. Unlike many of the psychiatrists who were passing off drugs as my cure, I was not conning myself. I was indulging and damaging myself, yes, but I was not deceiving myself by thinking it was good for me when I chose to use drugs.

People in trouble need to have the freedom to take prescribed medication or not. My choice is firm—I will pass. Having said that, if you choose to take antidepressants, do so in good conscience. Appreciate the fact that you are allowing yourself to accept help. Accepting outside help can at times be a lifesaver.

I have had trauma in my life, and I still have difficult feelings related to those times. But rather than try to block out those difficult feelings by numbing myself, I now understand that feelings are temporary, and so I am able to live through them knowing that they will pass. With this understanding, I am now much better equipped to handle the challenges that earlier led me into the cycle of drinking myself into oblivion and then seeking out psychiatric solutions.

Having had debilitating depression and suicidal tendencies throughout my life, I can understand why someone would say that medication is at least better than suicide. That is true. And of all people, I understand the need for relief from depression. So I am not saying that it is wrong or bad to help yourself by taking prescribed medication. I am just saying that as you make that choice, you need to know there may be a much more satisfying solution.

To many people, I was a lost cause in my misery, and so they believed that I was doomed to therapy and prescriptions as my only cure. They were wrong.

Several times in my years of struggle, I tried to commit suicide. Each time I came dangerously close to ending my own life and I landed in a hospital emergency room. And each time, I was *already on several antidepressants*. So, obviously, antidepressant drugs are not always effective in helping people choose life over suicide.

Depression is more complex than what just the simple popping of a pill can fix. It is not necessarily bad to take pills; I just do not see them as a real solution for depression.

I actually had two car accidents while loaded up on various antidepressants and other prescription mood stabilizers. None of the doctors had told me that I should not drive while taking the drugs. They did not even tell me to be careful. In fact, one doctor knew I was driving all over Los Angeles every day while I was taking the drugs he prescribed for me.

One accident that I had was on the busy 101 freeway on a day, believe it or not, when the traffic was actually moving pretty fast. The first person I called from the side of the road—a man I trusted to take care of me—expressed more concern about the psychiatrist than about my safety. The first thing he said to me was, *"Don't say anything—the doctor could lose his license!"*

The point is that you need to be intelligent about the choices you make. In the *business* of medicine, it is becoming increasingly important to pay attention to your *true needs* so that you are more likely to receive appropriate and adequate care. Because we are constantly bombarded with remedies—often from people who do not have our best interests at heart—it is more important now than ever that we understand what our true needs really are. Perhaps when it comes to depression, our true needs revolve more around matters of the *heart* rather than matters of the *brain*.

⌘

Chapter 7

UGLY

"The secret of ugliness consists
not in irregularity,
but in being uninteresting"

Ralph Waldo Emerson

As far back as I can remember, I have felt ugly physically and ugly inside, as a person. Yes, I was a model, but if you were to see my pictures, there are only one or two shots with a smile—and those did not even make it into my portfolio. I did not feel gorgeous, as some people said I was, and I definitely did not feel as beautiful as the other girls.

I felt like a fake. I had been kicked out of public school at fourteen, and by the time I was sixteen, I had slept with more guys than I could count on both my hands and my feet—twice. I felt dirty and ashamed. I had the history of using drugs and alcohol. I had the drug and alcohol rehabs. I had the eating disorders. *Beautiful* girls did not do any of that.

Yet I put on a face for the world to see. I felt like I always put on a face—except when I was kicking back with a drink and a smoke. It was only then that I was able to comfortably be me. That is a large reason why changing my habits was so difficult. I had been using alcohol, drugs and cigarettes for so long that I was extremely uncomfortable when I was without them. Without my habits I felt like I was trapped in someone else's skin, someone I did not know. *"Who is this person?"* *"I can't live like this."* *"How will people know who I am?"* Thoughts and feelings like that would go through my mind, and I would really miss my old habits. I missed my groove. I did not think that I could be anything but this "using" identity because, as far as I knew, this identity was me.

In the beginning, when I first quit drinking and smoking and I felt this way, I would remind myself of the horrifying experience of withdrawal that I went through during my last detox. During that torture I could care less about any feelings I had for my "groove," or about people knowing who I was. At that moment what I truly cared about was my sanity and my life.

The unfamiliar person, the *me* without the drugs, was someone I just needed to get used to. There was nothing to do but just to do it.

That transition, however, was not as long or as difficult as I had feared. Of course, I still have the occasional drinking or smoking impulse, but later on, after that old familiar desire has passed, I am always pleased—and relieved—that I did not follow through on that impulse to be my old identity.

I think the desire to hang on to one's old identity is why some people have trouble letting go of their addictions. I would often notice this phenomenon in recovery meetings, and I feel that it is a large road block to recovery.

When we hold on to our old identity, we remain unchanged in many crucial ways. An example of this would be constantly talking about getting high. If we do that, we are teasing ourselves with temptation, which usually leads a person back to use—or at least to the frustrations of always yearning to.

Another example of holding on to an old identity would be adopting a "been there, done that" attitude, with the feeling that there is nothing more to learn, that we have done it all. This often holds people in the same frame of mind as when they were using, and it usually limits their capacity to have new inner experiences of change and growth, which are essential for a successful recovery.

It was not enough for me to just stop ingesting substances. I had spent the greater part of my life heavily drinking and smoking, and in doing so I missed out on opportunities to know other aspects of my personality. As soon as I quit using, I was free to get to know those other parts of myself.

However, in order to truly get to know those other aspects of my personality, I had to be willing to let go of my old self as I knew it. It was necessary for me to release my identification with my old habits in order to discover the more fascinating sides of myself that now help me maintain my current well-being and healthy habits.

In order to have a strong base to support new healthy behaviors, I believe that we have to let go of not only the *physical* habits that have caused us so much trouble, but also the *psychological* habits that go along with them.

It can be difficult to release one's identity, but it is not impossible. For over twenty years I believed that I was limited, damaged and ugly.

Because of those negative beliefs about myself, it was much easier for me to accept my heavy drinking and smoking. It did not matter that those choices were not serving me well because that was who I thought I was.

But I was wrong. It turns out that the old identity, the heavy drinker-smoker person, was merely all that I could *see*. When I freed myself from my old habits, I was able to notice many other not-so-dreary parts of my personality that were actually interesting and even kind of fun.

As more time passes without drinking and as my thinking becomes clearer, I have become more and more satisfied with new aspects of my personality and also with areas of life that were not at all interesting to me before. It was not too long after I let go of my old habits and was able to get *outside* of my old identity that my natural interest in life emerged—often without my even noticing.

No longer burdened by the physical and mental weight of addictive habits, I started to feel a genuine interest in things other than those which revolved around satisfying those habits. Once my brain was finally allowed the opportunity to think clearly, I was able to notice new realities. And one of those realities is that I no longer exclusively experience myself as that old, ugly identity I once believed was me.

In my substance-abusing life, I had become bored. Although I was doing most of the basic tasks that life requires, I was uninspired. All that I knew about life depressed me. All that I knew about myself saddened, angered and disappointed me. I was living in a very narrow world, and that reflected upon my opinion of myself. I bottled up all those dismal and dreary feelings of mine, and I used them to define myself. That is how I ended up ugly in my mind.

Looking back, I can see that it is not so much that I found life itself uninteresting and boring, although I had often thought so, or that people found *me* uninteresting and boring, although I'm sure that in my drunkenness some people did. What I can see now is that I had become uninteresting and boring *to myself.* That left me open and vulnerable to all of my negative self-criticisms, including the big one—that I was bad and ugly.

To change that low opinion of myself—to change my alcohol-guzzling, cigarette-smoking identity—it was necessary that I quit ingesting those things, of course, but it was also just as important that I allow myself to have *new* thoughts and opinions about myself as well as about life.

In the following passage you can see how an

identity might be formed and how we can create a more personally interesting and meaningful sense of identity. This passage is attributed to many sources (of which I will choose "Chinese Proverb"), and it is worth a good look:

> *Thoughts become words.*
> *Words become actions.*
> *Actions become habits.*
> *Habits become character.*
> *And character becomes your destiny.*

This is a good explanation of how our negative habits and beliefs develop. It also shows how our destiny can be altered by changing our thoughts.

⌘

Chapter 8

DREAD

"I don't ever want to feel like I did that day.
Take me to the place I love, take me all the way."

Under the Bridge
Red Hot Chili Peppers

*I*n my life-long search for help and support in the healing of my addictions and depression, I have been involved with many different types of therapy. Aside from massage therapy, what I enjoyed the most was group therapy.

That was true regardless of the facilitator—whether it was a doctor, a therapist or a volunteer patient. I actually enjoyed observing the other people in the group and listening to them talk about their struggles. Not only was it a relief to have the focus be on someone else for a while, but it was also of benefit for me when I was able to notice my own patterns that were similar to theirs.

By listening to someone else in the group therapy sessions talk about their struggle with a problem that was similar to my own, I was able to take a step back and think about the problem objectively, without my own emotions and feelings clouding my view. On occasion, by listening carefully as others brooded over their problems, I was better able to understand my own difficulties and even to make some positive adjustments in my behavior.

However, in spite of my appreciation for the group therapy process, there was a troubling aspect to it that I found was mirrored in my own private therapy sessions. In the group process it was not the similarities between me and the other patients that disturbed me—it was something I saw in the group facilitators as well as in my own private therapists. It was a method that many of them used to attempt to facilitate healing and growth that seemed to be a lot like a dog chasing its own tail.

While participating in group therapy, when I was not in the "hot seat," I was better able to observe the dynamics that occurred between the patient and the facilitator. What I noticed was an unsettling and discouraging approach to healing difficult emotions. We were told that, in order to heal, we must focus on and dissect events and circumstances of our past. For instance, this meant that if I wanted to heal, I would need to discuss the sexual abuse that my grandfather inflicted upon me when I was a small girl. Or, if I preferred, I could focus on my mother having abandoned me and my siblings when I was five years old.

What I can tell you about this is that, in my nearly 30 years of therapy, I have discussed *every* detail of my childhood more times than I can count—again and again and again. Yet during all those years of therapy that focused on my past, I still suffered intensely. And for most of those 30 years, even as I was hashing and rehashing my past in therapy, I continued to drink daily, smoke constantly, throw up, starve myself, and ruthlessly behave in many other self-destructive ways. There comes a point at which discussion of past events becomes useless—when it is time to stop chasing our tails.

No one, including myself, ever seemed to be "all better" from therapy. I understand, of course, that "all better" may be asking too much, as there is always room for more learning and personal growth in our lives. But I do not believe that asking for a major improvement in one's life from psychotherapy—group or private—is asking for too much at all.

I do believe that it is important to *express* feelings and fears related to our past, and I am bothered when I hear things like, "Get over it." "The past is over." "Grow up." "Move on." Some of the things I experienced in my past were really bad, and I understand the value of expressing my hurt and disappointment regarding those experiences. I want to stand up for myself and announce that it's just not okay to hurt people in that way. On the other hand, there is benefit in the *idea* of letting go of the past.

Some of us have suffered greatly in childhood and we need to share those experiences in order to heal feelings of shame and unworthiness. However, I believe it is a misconception that those traumas are at the root of our suffering. I believe our suffering has more to do with our *current* feelings about those experiences than with the actual events of the past.

What I am suggesting is that past experiences—no matter how wrong, painful and torturous they may have been—do not cause our bad feelings in the present. Of course you will want to—as you should—share your traumatic and terrible experiences from your past, but in doing so it is important to remember that it is your *feelings* about those experiences that are causing you difficulty today, not the actual experiences themselves. Those experiences have ended. However, for some people this step of sharing past experiences is essential in order to break through shameful feelings and feelings of unworthiness.

Even so, to over-focus on past negative experiences can actually hinder the process of healing our negative feelings in the present. It can also interfere with the discovery of our inner power, strength and goodness.

The tendency to over-focus on painful events in the past is what I observed in both private therapy and group therapy sessions. We would go over and over an event or circumstance of the past, usually something from childhood. We would cover every angle of the event, being sure to ask the ever so important question, "And how did that make you feel?" That *is* an important question, but if further healing steps are not taken, then asking that question only serves to leave us feeling poorly— or whatever it was that we were feeling regarding the event in question.

Discussing the actual event, and the trauma of it, is one step, but it is only one step. I believe that the more important step for overcoming trauma and emotional difficulties is something altogether different. In my experience, when I focused on the *feeling* that an event aroused and worked to *release* that feeling, I had much more success in solving my problems than when I would concentrate on what actually happened.

What I noticed in group therapy was that we all had nearly identical difficulties and struggles with drugs, alcohol, sex, food and depression, yet we all had different backgrounds. One person might have been beaten by his father; another, sexually molested; and another, abandoned in a foster home. However, in spite of our different circumstances and events of the past, we each had the same *feelings* of suffering and despair in the present. When I realized this, I understood that the important thing is not the specific events of the past, because they can be different for each of us, but the similar response we each have in the present of feelings of suffering and despair.

That is why I believe true liberation from emotional torment is not going to be achieved in the countless hours of therapy that simply hash and rehash the details of our past events. Instead, therapy should help us live through the feelings of the present—no matter how long we have carried those feelings. When we understand those feelings cannot harm us, we will no longer be afraid of experiencing them. That is emotional freedom.

It took me a long time to learn this lesson, with no thanks to psychotherapy. When I was younger (and in therapy) I always referred to my emotionally traumatic pain as the "bubble feeling." That is the pain I always thought, especially as a child, that only *I* experienced. I used to wish that my mom or my dad or any of my therapists could live inside of me for just one second so they could know what I was trying so desperately to explain. I thought that if any one of them could experience what I suffered every moment of every day, then surely they would not hesitate to come and save me. That person would understand the torture that I lived with and would instantly do everything possible to rescue me.

I remember that as a child, even during the times when I was allowed to see my mother, all I could think about was when I would have to leave her again. I was constantly agonizing and worrying during our short visits together.

The "mature" person would have said (and they did), *"That's hours from now, Amy. Enjoy the time that you've got."*

That did *not* make me feel any better. In fact,

I felt worse. Now, not only was I terrified of the inevitable separation, but I also felt guilty, inadequate and wrong for not being able to "enjoy the moment" as I was expected to.

I recall on several occasions locking myself in my mother's bathroom right before I had to leave her. I would cry hysterically. But there was a good reason for that—I was terrified. I was afraid of returning home, where I would be frightened at night when everyone was in bed and I was wide awake and feeling absolutely alone. I was not afraid of the dark, or of some imaginary monster in the closet or under my bed. I was terrified of something that I had no name for—an overwhelming emotional monster I lived with every day for a very long time.

I began to feel as if I were living in a bubble—a painful, blurry feeling of separation between myself and everyone else. As the night came on, my feelings of isolation magnified into panic. Since almost every moment was agony to get through, I developed the terrible habit of needing to "get through" time, which is why it never appealed to me to try to "be" in the moment. I was desperately trying to get through the moment, not to be in it.

When I was eleven, and for almost the entire

school year of my sixth grade, the feeling of panic was so strong I could not sleep in my own room. So I often slept on the floor in the hallway with my head lying near my sister's bedroom door.

That was the year when I first began seriously contemplating suicide. I remember several times going into the kitchen and holding a large knife to my stomach, wondering if I could do it. I also went into the bathroom several times and laid on the floor with whatever bottle of pills was in the medicine cabinet, trying to feel what it would be like to be dead. Would it be better?

It is difficult to explain precisely what came over me then—and periodically thereafter throughout my life—that terrified me so deeply. It was a feeling of extreme panic and doom. It was a feeling that I have dreaded always. Again, that is *the bubble feeling.*

In working to overcome my addictions and to heal the terrible feelings that led me to constantly inebriate myself, I have discovered that I have choices. I can focus only on the disturbing events of my past, believing that is the way to emotional freedom. But if I really want to make a difference in my healing and happiness, I can do what I have done. And that is to face the bubble feeling head on, because it is that feeling—triggered by painful events—that is at the root of so much of my suffering.

Just thinking about how terrifying that feeling was when I was a child can still make me shudder. And the bubble feeling will always be in my memory. But it does not, and will not, have any sort of control or power over me, as I used to believe that it had. It was a terrible, sickening, horrible, long-lasting feeling, but still…it was only a feeling. And feelings cannot actually harm us.

Whenever there is a threat of any kind, including an emotional threat, people instinctively want to run. But that's not always the best response. Some people find healthy ways to respond, and some people, like I used to be, are overwhelmed and they reach for anything to save them—anything like alcohol, drugs, food, or sex.

Until I actually dealt with my bubble feeling, the more I avoided it, the scarier and bigger it became. As a young teenager, I had vowed that I would never, ever allow myself to suffer what I had suffered through in the sixth grade and so I began the habit of avoiding the "bubble feeling." But in my confusion, I was doing the exact opposite of what would have helped me. Because I did not yet understand how to work with my emotions, instead of living through the bubble feeling and learning for myself that it could not harm me, I tried to completely avoid it by numbing myself with drugs and alcohol. I made that vow to protect myself from my horrible feelings, but by refusing to face those feelings, I unknowingly tied myself closer to them. In this way, I was digging myself into a deeper hole of addiction, depression, and misery.

⌘

Chapter 9

DESIRE

"I want you. I want you so bad,
it's driving me mad, it's driving me mad."

I Want You (She's So Heavy)
The Beatles

*I*mmediate gratification. There. Now you know what this chapter is about. When releasing addictions, it is extremely helpful to understand the difference between the desires of your true nature and desires related to immediate gratification.

As I have healed, I have come to love and respect my capacity to desire. In my addiction I hated it. I cursed the fact that I seemed to be insatiable and incapable of ever feeling satisfied. I always sought more and more pleasure—more drink, more smoke, more food, and more of whatever it was that day or that hour that gave me some immediate gratification. I always desired more. I had been told that I drank like a fish or that I was a bottomless pit, and I had to agree. I was never full.

What I did not understand was that I was wrong to condemn desire and to criticize myself for having strong desires. I had not yet learned to distinguish the true desires of my nature for goodness, joy, and love from my strong desires for immediate gratification through alcohol, cigarettes, food or whatever else I thought I needed right that second.

What I understand now is that desire itself is not a bad or wrong thing. Some of the things I desired in the past were not always so great, but I have discovered that desire itself is actually a great thing. Desire fuels creation. We need desire to live a full life.

But I know now that I don't need *all* of the things I have desired and taken in the past. Many of those things—alcohol, cigarettes, drugs, food, indiscriminate sex—were not what I *truly* desired anyway. They only *felt* as if they were in that moment. After I had fed one of those strong desires and that moment of temporary satisfaction had ended, the desire would immediately begin to

grow again. It never ended for me, and it continued until I finally understood the nature of my *true*
desires and went about fulfilling those instead.

I have found the *process* of working to fulfill
my true desires to be as satisfying, invigorating and
inspiring as actually *achieving fulfillment* of those
desires—although achievement is great too. When
I choose immediate gratification, I miss the
genuinely gratifying process of working to satisfy
the desires of my true nature.

When learning to satisfy our *true* desires, it's
important to be able to recognize what those true
desires are—and what they are not. We all have
the natural desire to eat and drink; we obviously
could not sustain our bodies otherwise. However,
we do not have the *natural* desire to consume two
large pizzas, a gallon of ice cream, and a case of
beer—although for some, that may *feel* like a
natural desire, but it's actually one that has been
confused and distorted.

For example, if a person deeply desires love in
their life and they mistake sex for love and then
only desire sex, they have confused and missed out
on their true desire, which was for love.

The point is that desires can be distorted.
Therefore, it's important to become familiar with
our true desires so we can know when we are

distorting them as opposed to beneficially satisfying them.

When I would have a strong desire for a drink, I didn't consciously think or feel, *"I want feelings of warmth from another person. I wish to feel nurtured."* Instead, I thought, *"Man, I want a drink—now."* But if I had suddenly been swept over by an overwhelming feeling of being deeply nurtured, cared for, and loved, then all desire for that drink would have immediately vanished in me.

Constantly masking "true desires" with "immediate gratification" makes it difficult to have the patience to slow down and discover what our true desires really are.

Even though my family was not wealthy, I grew up with my own telephone, my own television, and I had a car at sixteen. When people really want something, they can usually find a way to get it—and I did. Drugs, alcohol, and cigarettes were some of the easier things for me to get. I had to get a fake ID for some things, and I had to sleep around for other things, but I almost always managed to get what I wanted when I wanted it.

With all that we have available to fulfill our desires, it really is up to each of us to personally monitor ourselves. Since we are each our own boss when deciding what to do with our desires, it's important we learn to distinguish the desires of our true nature from the desires that can't give us what we *really* want. To help make this distinction, we can ask ourselves: *Is this desire coming from an unhealthy place of fear and insecurity, or is it coming from a healthy place of truth, love and nurturing?*

⌘

Chapter 10

ℒOVE

"Self-love, my liege
Is not so vile a sin as self-neglecting."

William Shakespeare

W hen I think about a typical self-help book, this is what I hear: *"You come first. You must learn to love yourself first."* I never cared for such statements. I always thought the idea of "love yourself first" was a selfish and self-centered one. In fact, I did not find the idea of loving myself meaningful until I unknowingly began to practice it during my last detox.

Have you ever been really sick and your mother (or someone) tucked you in bed with whatever you needed—something soothing to eat, like soup or tapioca, a good book or magazine, and the TV remote? I missed out on much of that myself, but I experienced it enough to know that there are certain good feelings of surrender and pleasure that come when you are taken care of in that way.

When I was suffering intensely during my last horrible detox, I took a lot of hot showers whenever I could. I was cold and sweaty all the time, so it was good to clean up, but I also happen to love hot showers. When I was done with my shower, I would put on a comfy T-shirt and crawl back into bed with my fluffy blanket and pillows all around me. Then I would just lie there, doing nothing. That can be hard to do without feeling guilty for wasting the day away, but I had to do it. I was really sick and frightened, and my body was in a state of shock. I *needed* to be in bed. And even though I didn't realize it at the time, I was inadvertently learning to love myself as I lay in my bed, feeling miserable.

By taking a hot shower, which was pleasurable, by putting on my most comfortable clothes, also pleasurable, and by lying in bed, I ceased demanding anything of myself, and I surrendered to the process of detoxing. I was caring for myself. I *felt* horrible physically, emotionally, and mentally, but at the same time, I knew I was doing the right thing because I also felt slightly safe and protected.

I never would have thought I had the capacity to comfort myself in that way. That was me *learning to love myself.* Surprisingly, at the time that did not seem selfish or self-centered to me. It seemed to be absolutely mandatory because my body was shot. I had been running on empty for so many years that it was amazing I was even still alive.

However, when people are depleted the way I was—physically, mentally, and emotionally—they don't usually realize they are depleted since it comes on very slowly. For them, depletion feels natural.

I had been running around and pushing myself daily for so many years I didn't realize that much of my struggle was due to body/mind depletion. If, rather than thinking I had some "baffling" disease, I had instead understood that much of my distress was coming from having a depleted body, I could have done something about it—once I learned how to love myself.

After all of the trouble that I had caused myself and others for so much of my life, I did not believe I deserved any kind of a break. But once I convinced myself that it was okay to rest for a while, my body absolutely jumped at the opportunity to slow down and take a break. When I first stopped drinking and smoking, I stayed in bed, sleeping on and off for more than a week. I was that beat. Thank goodness my circumstances at the time allowed me to do that.

That small step of allowing my body to rest was, in truth, a *monumental* step towards loving myself. Once I began to relax a little—and a little was all that was possible for me during that anguish—my self-care did not feel like selfishness. It felt like *kindness*.

I decided that I could accept that kind of approach to "loving myself." I even discovered that loving myself in that gentle way—that is, simply by being kind to myself—was actually very nice.

I had spent most of my life neglecting myself. Sure, I constantly poured alcohol and other substances down my throat, always making sure that I was nearly drowning in whatever I might be taking, but that was feeding my fear and nervousness, not helping my body, mind, or emotions. It was not feeding me—*my spirit, my soul, my self.* Saturating myself with substances was my mistaken attempt to numb my confused and painful emotions. But it was my spirit that was hungry. It was my true self that was hungry for self-love, for self-care, and for self-kindness.

This was all new to me, but I was determined to learn it because it seemed to be a crucial element in healing my addictive patterns and habits.

Perhaps because I was without a mother for a great deal of my childhood, or perhaps because the sky is blue—whatever the reason may be—I did not learn to properly nurture and care for myself. Instead, I adopted a demanding, harsh and impatient attitude. So, during my last detox, I was essentially forced to calm and nurture myself and begin proper self-care. Since I was not accustomed to taking care of myself, it was difficult for me to accept my own kindness. In fact, in the beginning of my healing, I felt so unworthy, guilty and bad about myself that I didn't feel as if I deserved any kindness at all.

I remember in the movie "Ferris Bueller's Day Off" how adorable I thought Mathew Broderick was when he was pretending to be sick. His mother was doting all over him, and he shamelessly soaked it up as he lay in bed. I felt I could never do that for myself because I would feel too uncomfortable being showered with kind words of affection and care. So when I was able to allow myself to enjoy an extended rest in my own bed, I was healing not only my body but my heart as well.

It is nearly impossible to overcome addictive habits if you cannot learn to be kind to yourself. In my own healing I have learned the truth of that. No matter what positive changes I tried to make, if I continued to criticize and condemn myself, I always resorted to my old familiar negative habits—always. It was only when I began to adopt a relaxed manner of being kind to myself that I was able to have the patience necessary to move forward with my new, healthier habits.

⌘

Chapter 11

ℬLISTERS

"The record shows I took the blows,
And I did it my way!"

My Way
Frank Sinatra

Not too long after I quit drinking, I was visiting my mother. Since I didn't have a bike—my latest form of exercise—I decided to take a walk. I was putting on my shoes, and she asked, "Don't you want to put on some socks? It's really hot. You'll get blisters."

"Nah," I said, "I hate socks. Anyway, these are new shoes. They're supposed to be aerodynamic or something."

"Well, at least take a couple of Band Aids with you just in case," she added.

I didn't think I would need any, but I decided

to take a few anyway.

I had not even made it to my halfway mark when the first blister began forming—and hurting. I stopped and put a Band Aid on my right ankle, and a block later I put a Band Aid on my left ankle.

By the time I made it to the drugstore, my feet were hurting so badly that I could barely walk. I purchased a box of extra-thick Band Aids and doubled up on each ankle. That did not help.

I must have looked pretty ridiculous limping home on both legs, but worse than that, the blisters really hurt! I would have gone barefoot, but the temperature outside was nearly one-hundred degrees that day and the pavement would have been too hot to bear.

I made it back to my mother's with my tail slightly between my legs. I immediately took off my shoes, and I swore I would think twice about any potentially helpful advice offered to me, particularly when it's coming from someone with a pretty good track record.

I usually automatically resist advice, thinking that I always know what is best for me. But once again, I saw that I do not *always* know what is best for me—a great deal of the time maybe, but not always.

I was twenty years old when I got my D.U.I. citation. My friends and I often hung out after work at a bar in Calabasas, for drinks and dancing. It was down the road from the restaurant where we worked together. We all knew the police had been out a lot lately, and with many successful D.U.I. arrests, we knew to be careful.

To me, however, being careful meant watching for the cops, not watching how much I drank. Apparently I did not do either. I blew an alcohol blood level of 0.15 when they pulled me over—which, being the drinker that I was, was not especially high, but for driving it was way over the legal limit.

I spent that night in the lovely Van Nuys jail.

Later, there were some stiff consequences from that night. I lost my driver's license for quite a while. I also had to pay high fines for the ticket itself as well as pay for a series of alcohol education classes that I really did not want to attend. I was also ordered to attend a lot of AA meetings—which by that time in my life I already knew was not going to help me.

I knew that drunk driving was something to be avoided. I knew that it was dangerous and sometimes deadly. Prior to my arrest I knew the consequences of a drunk driving arrest were extreme. Several of my friends had gotten D.U.I.'s before me. I knew about Mothers Against Drunk Driving and their campaign against the deadly dangers of drunk driving. I knew a lot—but what I didn't know was that I did not know *everything*. I did not know when to stop believing that I was always right and when to take someone's caution seriously.

Just as I could have listened to my mom and taken two seconds to put on a pair of socks to avoid a week of painful blisters, I could have taken the two seconds it takes to interrupt my old, familiar thought patterns with a new thought, such as, "*Hey, maybe I could arrange a ride first.*"

I might have considered that driving after drinking too much was not just about me and my desire to do whatever I wanted. It also potentially involved other people and other lives. I also could have thought that I did not need the added pain or trouble of a D.U.I. in my own life, which I certainly did not.

My thought process—or lack thereof—was the same the night that I got arrested as it was the day that I got the blisters. I did what I wanted to do without pausing to think ahead. Obviously, in both cases it would have been much wiser if I had thought about the consequences of the choices I was making.

The point is that no one is always right. It's important to look at a situation from all angles as best we can. When making our decisions, large or small, we can question the advice of others as well as our own self-advice. No matter who you are or what you are doing, it is always beneficial to take a moment to consider that you might be wrong before committing to an important decision. When you are in a situation that involves making a choice, it might help you to briefly step back and ask yourself, "*Do I really want blisters?*"

⌘

Chapter 12

CONDEMNED

"You yourself, as much as anybody in the entire universe, deserve your love and affection."

Buddha

When I was a teenager there were many times when someone's parents would go out of town and leave the kids in charge of the house. When that happened my friends and I would go on a drinking, drugging, and sexing binge that would last for days. It was not unusual to find someone passed out on the couch or on the floor. We were extreme in our behaviors, and we thought we were having a lot of fun.

Later on, as my friends decided that other things in life were more interesting or more important than having these all-night binges, they moved on. I decided to find other friends who wanted to keep on partying with me.

As I grew older, the partying got more sophisticated than when I was a punked out teenaged rebel, but it was really the same process of getting wasted and getting laid. I just wore a prettier dress.

At that time, I did not have the vision of a house with a white picket fence and a husband who wanted 2.5 kids—or any kids, for that matter. Some people might say that was a good thing, given my self-absorbed, unhealthy behaviors. But my reluctance to be a parent was more about avoiding pain than it was about not wanting a child. I was not interesting in experiencing the emotional rollercoaster I feared went along with having a child. I had already deeply suffered the agony of loss in a parent-child relationship, and I did not want to risk facing that pain again.

Drinking, drugging, and numbing my feelings had allowed me to avoid feeling some of the pain of loss—but not always. And when that pain hit, it hit hard. Sometimes I would be so overwhelmed by my intense fear and despair that I could not even numb myself with the usual drink or drugs. When that happened, in a panic, I would physically hurt myself by cutting my arms, or I would run to a friend's house or to my mother's house to sleep on her couch. At times I ended up in some sort of hospital where I would anxiously ride out my panic until I felt well enough to drink and smoke again. I had been using substances for so long that they were my main inspiration for getting out of bed to face the day.

I know that all the years of drugs (including the prescribed ones), daily consumption of huge amounts of alcohol, and malnutrition all contributed to the intensity and exaggeration of my negative emotions. But when I was experiencing those terrifying feelings of panic and despair, it made no difference to me what had caused them—they felt unbearable regardless.

However, as I gained some clarity and balance in my life, I became curious to understand how I came to that place of such deep turmoil, despair and panic. I was not interested in blaming anyone, and I understood that insight into the past is not the same as healing in the present. However, I was curious to understand how I ended up so sad.

In my search for answers I came to understand that what I needed above all during my years of emotional turmoil was to feel and to be *safe*. The other issues were secondary, or even irrelevant. If my circumstances had allowed me to feel some degree of emotional safety, it's much more likely that I would have behaved in healthier ways.

Although I behaved as if I didn't care what I thought about myself, obviously I did care. I was listening to my every thought, and every word to myself was that I was *bad*. I treated myself the same way we treat criminals—*very badly*.

In my search and discovery, I have come to learn that if we are hoping to help a person to change and heal, negative judgment and harsh treatment is absolutely the wrong way to do that. I recently heard a short segment of a prominent radio host's call-in advice show. A mother called in to ask the female "expert" for advice about her pregnant, twenty-seven-year-old, alcoholic daughter who already had two babies, one of which had Fetal Alcohol Syndrome. The radio host's advice was to forget the "scummy daughter."

What troubled me was that the radio host, who was in a position of authority, showed no compassion for the daughter or for the caller, who was clearly hurting over her daughter's behavior. The mother had called seeking help, and the radio host encouraged her to feel anger and judgment. It bothered me that a person in an authoritative position seemed to advise out of an anger reaction, and it concerned me that someone truly seeking help might trustingly follow the advice of that person.

Of course the babies of the alcoholic mother needed help. Clearly that was a situation that needed to be dealt with. But the advice that was given was hateful and one-sided. The "expert" forgot the young alcoholic mother was a suffering human being who also needed help. *She was also a daughter.*

Condemnation is not a tool for health or healing. Condemnation causes more fear, more blame, and consequently more turmoil. Although that young mother will suffer the consequences of her choices, as will her children, she is not a hopeless person because alcohol led her to lose her grip on life. She may act stupid, cruel and careless, but she is a suffering, struggling human being who needs help. It does the world, her children, and herself no good for an angry radio talk show host to condemn her as a "scummy daughter."

If the mother followed the host's advice and treated her daughter as scum, it would only intensify the negative feelings that are at the core of the daughter's problems. Condemnation and criticism by others would make it more difficult for her to rise above her own self-condemning thoughts that she must certainly have, given the depth of her drinking.

If people just criticize her behavior, leaving

her feeling horrible and doomed—which is what the radio host angrily and hatefully recommended—the situation would most likely continue to deteriorate. On the other hand, if the daughter could be treated with love and understanding, then there would be hope for healing and change. With healing and change, she is more likely to be a better mother to the children the caller was concerned for.

As a result of my own heavy drinking, I know what it's like to feel unsafe, unworthy, horrible and doomed. During my own dark days when I constantly condemned and criticized myself, what I most needed to help me change my self-destructive ways was not added criticism but a feeling of safety that only kindness, compassion and love can inspire.

Everyone is worthy of love. Drugs, alcohol and even criminal behaviors do not make a person unworthy of love. Some people might be unwanted, disgusting, and even possibly dangerous, but they are *never* unworthy of love. If we can understand that, then perhaps our difficulties will no longer be so difficult.

⌘

Chapter 13

ℬELIEF

"Every Warrior of the Light has suffered for the most trivial of reasons. Every Warrior of the Light has, at least once, believed he was not a Warrior of the Light."

Paulo Coelho

ℬecause our beliefs guide our choices, what we believe is extremely important in our lives. However, in the same way your desires can be distorted, so too can your beliefs be distorted.

For example, if I believe, as I so often did in my past, that I am going to have a miserable night alone unless I get some alcohol to spice up the evening, then most likely I would choose to drink because, in accordance with my belief, I would be miserable otherwise.

What we believe is important because our beliefs influence our experience. If we hold negative beliefs about life, then our experience of life tends to be negative. I know this from personal experience. In the past I believed that I was bad because I drank, smoked, and had a lot of promiscuous sex. I believed I was bad because I did not finish school and my parents were divorced. I believed I was bad because I moved a lot and I didn't have lifelong friends like some people have. I believed I was bad because I was unhappy. I believed I was ugly—physically and spiritually. I believed all of the unkind thoughts that I had ever had about myself. Being locked into those extremely negative beliefs, you can understand the difficulty I had trying to improve my life.

When I gave up my destructive physical habits, I found it helpful to learn to view my negative thoughts and beliefs in the same way that I had come to view my drinking—as a long-term *habit*. Like any other habit, the habit of creating negative beliefs can be changed. Beliefs can be altered, adjusted, or abandoned.

Of course, changing a habit of any kind, particularly a habit of belief, is not easy. It takes determination and practice. It also requires plenty of positive reinforcement—usually and most beneficially your own. Just remember that even though negative mental habits *can* be changed, it may not be any easier to do so than it is to change negative physical habits. It's easy to see when your negative physical habit leads you to pick up a cigarette, but it is not as easy to see when your negative mental habit leads you to diminish yourself.

Once I was able to understand and accept that the goodness and value of me—or of life in general—did not disappear simply because I had terrible feelings about myself—or about life—then I was able to make even greater changes than just stopping my substance abuse. With the new understanding that my negative feelings do not alter the true goodness of me as a person, I was able to believe that there might be something in me worth saving, some reason for me to make difficult, monumental changes in my life. I became much more willing to examine my old, nearly lifelong negative beliefs about myself and about life. I was able to consider that perhaps my beliefs had been distorted by my intense and overwhelming negative feelings.

I feel there is an underlying goodness in life. That core goodness did not cease to exist simply because I believed that life is horrible and bad. The core goodness of life is not changed by what we feel or even by what we do. People can behave in ways that are abusive, self-centered, greedy and stupid, but those behaviors do not change the innate goodness of life or of each of us. Those negative behaviors grow out of our confused or negative *beliefs*.

This is a very inspiring and empowering way to think about life. If you are willing to believe there is an inherent goodness in you as a person, then even if you've been guzzling alcohol for a very long time, shooting up heroin, or hurting others, you can still tap into your inherent goodness and learn to change your behavior. This is because no matter how degraded your behavior has been, you have not damaged the core goodness of you. Your core goodness is a truth about you that never goes away, no matter what negative things you may say or do (although you might not have very many friends). At any time, you can choose to end your destructive behaviors and begin to experience that goodness inside you, which can then inspire you to make positive changes.

When we drown our bodies with alcohol, flood them with cigarette smoke, or overindulge in sex to avoid negative feelings, we are not reflecting the true core goodness of ourselves. We are reflecting our negative feelings, our distorted beliefs, and our confused desires.

Our inner worth and goodness are not determined by our habits—physical or mental. Our habits can alter our *experience* of our inner goodness, but they cannot alter our core goodness.

When I was abusing my body with drugs, alcohol and other careless behaviors, I did not change my core being, the essence of me. However, I sure *felt* and *believed* I had, and that I was a bad person. I now understand that my negative actions were separate from the core goodness of me.

This does not mean that destructive, harmful behavior is an acceptable way to treat oneself or others. It means that our core goodness is always with us, and we can choose at any time to reflect more of it in our thoughts, feelings and behaviors.

If I always think to myself how disgusting I was for wasting over twenty years of my life with addictions, it would be impossible for me to feel better about myself, as I do today. In your healing, it's important to separate your understanding of who you are in your truest nature from your bad feelings about your destructive habits and behaviors. If your behaviors are destructive, then you need to stop them so you can more easily believe—and therefore *feel*—that you are a good person.

It's always beneficial to congratulate yourself

when you make healthier choices for yourself. Constantly remind yourself that you are a wonderful person. That kind of self-support is essential when overcoming addictions and depression on your own. And when in doubt, *always* err on the side of self-appreciation.

⌘

Chapter 14

ENERGY

*"When choosing between two evils
I always like to choose the one I've never tried before."*

Mae West

Shortly before I quit drinking, I was watching a motorcycle show on some do-it-yourself channel on TV. It featured a guy who owned a motorcycle shop. During the interview it came out that he used to have a big drug habit. He said that when he quit using drugs, he had so much energy that he had to find something to do with it. He decided to use his energy to focus on something that he loved—motorcycles—and so he opened up his own bike shop.

If you have ever quit using drugs or alcohol—or any psychologically or physically addictive habit—then you know you will usually have an overwhelming amount of "nervous" energy. That can feel maddening, especially if you don't have at least some understanding about it. Unfortunately, many people—including many of the professionals attempting to guide us—do not fully comprehend the positive nature of this nervous energy. They choose to try to get rid of it by sedating us with mood stabilizers or antidepressant drugs.

Although I can understand the desire to stop the troubling feelings that often accompany this nervous energy, I don't believe it's beneficial to do so because that nervous energy is actually an important part of our human nature. We don't need to experience that kind of energy as a bad feeling that we need to escape and overcome. It is a life-expressive energy that needs recognition, appreciation, and a place to go. I don't believe that nervous energy is part of the problem with staying sober. Just the opposite. That energy is a key to our healing. It can be our biggest ally when it's channeled into inspiring activities such as music, art, humane actions, and even motorcycles.

That guy on TV with the motorcycle shop intuitively knew he had to use his nervous energy or he would find himself using drugs again as a way to calm down. I don't know that he actually thought of it in that way, but I do know he embraced his energy rather than try to hide from it or make it go away. He channeled that strong energy into productive work with something he loved—motorcycles. He was obviously successful enough to be on that show, and he looked elated with life as they filmed him cruising down the highway on his Harley with his hair blowing in the wind.

At the time I saw that program, I was still drinking heavily, so I was way too exhausted to imagine that kind of accomplishment for myself. Even so, I was impressed by the way he used the nervous energy that arises when we stop drinking or drugging that I've never forgotten that man, always keeping the story of his success in the back of my mind. Not that I want to open my own motorcycle shop, but I do want to experience my positive desires and continue on with my own successes in the way I saw him doing in his life.

I have known many addicts in my life who were as beaten down as I was. In all of us there appeared to be a strong desire to express our energy, but there also appeared to be a heavy repression of that energy. I believe it's the repression of that energy and not the energy itself that leads us to destructive, numbing habits and behaviors and that many addictions start when the energy of our natural desire for a full life is smothered. And there are countless things that can smother that energy, including challenges with parents, social pressures, and of course, drugs and alcohol.

But no matter what we do or how drunk or high we get, we cannot truly kill our desire to live a full life. That desire exists to support us and to bring us joy—not to cause us difficulties.

It will help if you can understand your nervous energy as a beneficial life force that you can use to enhance your life and the lives of those around you. The problem is that when we stop coping and numbing with alcohol or drugs, that beneficial life force can begin to feel uncomfortable and even frightening. From my own experience of withdrawal, I know that the feeling of having pent-up nervous energy can be maddening and lead us to drink or take drugs in order to alleviate the uncomfortable feeling. But I also now understand that since such nervousness is an expression of our natural desire-energy, then that nervous energy is nothing to fear. It is actually something that can be used to serve us as we are learning new, healthier ways to fulfill our desire for joy in our lives.

Our desire-energy is a gift for us to use and benefit from in a positive way. When one attempts to suppress that energy just because it becomes nervous energy, it almost always causes a negative result. That negative result may be as small as a passing moment of disappointment, or it may be as large as a heroin overdose. By advising people with addictions or depression to avoid their desire-energy, or what appears to be negative nervous energy, I believe we are making a mistake. Desire-energy is a valuable tool even when it becomes the nervous energy that arises when we are ceasing our addiction. It does not serve us to view this energy as negative. It should be appreciated, understood, and directed in positive ways. We need to use it to our advantage rather than using it in ways that lead to our destruction.

⌘

Chapter 15

CRAVINGS

*"It is not the strongest of the species that survives,
nor the most intelligent,
but the one most responsive to change."*

Charles Darwin

*I*n your healing process there are several steps you can take when you feel you are in an emergency situation and that you cannot go on without a drink or a drug. However, no matter what you choose to do, it is important to understand that in the new healthy experiences you are trying to create, you are not trying to replicate the strong effects of alcohol or drugs.

Eventually, when all goes well in your healing process, you may be able to experience certain pleasurable feelings that you prefer over those of intoxication, but in the beginning, when you first give up an addictive habit, there is usually a period of adjustment that will be uncomfortable, and you may not have strong, positive feelings. If you know that this it is just part of the process of getting where you want to be, then you will also understand that such difficult experiences during the healing period will eventually pass. When you *temporarily* accept what in the moment feels less than all-satisfying and you put up the *least amount of resistance*, then you will find that any negative feelings that come up during the withdrawal period will come and go much more easily and more quickly.

When strong cravings arise, it feels like nothing can satisfy us but old destructive habits. I know that from experience. But I also know that in order to overcome addictions and long-held habits, you have to pass through the difficult feelings of not having the drink or drug that you desperately want and feel you need. This agonizing experience is a necessary part of withdrawing from addictions and long-held habits.

So if in healing we are going to have to go through these terrible feelings no matter what, then we should do all that we can to make the process more tolerable. Here are several suggestions I have found helpful in my own life.

First of all, there is no reason to make the process worse than it already might be. Now is the time to draw upon all of your kind, compassionate, and loving capacities and apply them to yourself. Be gentle with yourself, be understanding. Treat yourself as you would treat a child who needs to visit the dentist. Comfort yourself as much as possible, but go through the difficult experience anyway, trusting you will be the better for it.

You can also choose to understand your intense cravings for a destructive habit as a sign that you are on your way to getting better. Of course you will experience a strong desire when something you are attached to is taken away. In fact, if you don't have a strong response of craving, then perhaps you were not addicted. So rather than focusing on something you want but cannot have, try to view your craving as evidence that you are getting closer to what you *really* want, which is better health and freedom from the prison of addiction. *When you are having a craving, it means you are now in the healing process.*

It is important to remind yourself that the cravings you feel in the present will not last. You need to know there will come a time when you *will* feel better. So remind yourself of this often, because it's true. Ask anyone who has been through severe withdrawal or given up a long-held habit and they will tell you it gets much easier the further along you go in the healing process. So hang in there because it *can* be done.

It is also important to understand that after your body has completed whatever chemical withdrawal may be necessary, you are not going to die from a craving—no matter what you may *think*. Although it can *feel* like you are under attack, you are not in danger from a craving. Cravings come and go. Remind yourself that no matter how bad you feel, you will not die from a *feeling*. A feeling cannot harm you. It just feels bad in the moment.

Of course, just knowing intellectually that we can be in control of ourselves and our cravings is not always enough to regain the feeling of control. So sometimes we need additional help. If you are having a crisis and you feel that you cannot overcome your urges, then it may be necessary to find someone who can give you support.

If there is no available person or place you can physically go to for support, then call someone. If you cannot connect with anyone—as happened to me on many occasions—you can take a long, hot shower and get in bed with the curtains closed. Keep the TV remote nearby and distract yourself until the craving subsides and you feel well enough to move on, and hopefully connect with someone for support.

When you are feeling stronger, another thing to try—and you will want to make this a new habit as it will lend you much support in the future—is to learn to *question* your desires and impulses. For example, simply saying that you feel terrible because you are maniacally craving a drink is not going to help you to discover what you need to know in order to fully overcome your addictive habit. The real reason that you have the seemingly uncontrollable urge to drink is that you do not want to *feel* bad. It really is that simple. And of course, it is completely understandable to want to avoid feeling bad—most people do. However, in the case of withdrawal, sometimes we must allow ourselves to feel terrible for a period of time before we can feel good.

If you want to permanently get off the merry-go-round of addiction, you must be willing to ask yourself probing questions and dig for more meaningful answers about your cravings. You can ask yourself, "What *fear* is behind this craving?" For example, if you feel, "I've got to have a Bloody Mary this morning," you must learn not to take that feeling as final. Question that feeling. Ask yourself, "Do I crave tomato juice for some nutritional reason? No. Okay. Do I want a Bloody Mary because I *always* have one when I wake up and I'm craving it now simply out of habit? Yes. Interesting. Now that is something I can think more about." Or you might ask, "Are my hands shaking and I want them to stop, but I'm unwilling to ride out the withdrawal right now so that's why I want the drink?" If the answer is "yes," then you have something else that is important to think about.

By questioning your desires in this way, rather than just accepting a desire as the final answer, you can begin to distance yourself from the desire. Those initial questions are a good start because they can help us to see the real reason why we drink or use drugs. And the *real* reason is that we want to avoid painful negative feelings with the temporary distracting pleasure of inebriation.

If you go on in the questioning process, you can ask yourself this: "Is the real reason I want that Bloody Mary maybe because I feel that there is not enough joy and positive activity in my life? Am I afraid that there never will be enough joy in my life, so I will indulge myself now while I still can?"

When you are questioning yourself in this manner, it is important to do so without judgment against yourself. Questioning yourself is for the purpose of better understanding your responses and behaviors so that you can improve your life. It is not to find fault with yourself or to give you more opportunities for self-criticism. Question yourself as a wise observer would—with love, patience, compassion and, to the best of your ability, kind understanding.

When I first quit drinking, I found certain ways of thinking that helped ease me through tempting situations. For example, one night when my husband was playing guitar in a smoky little bar down the street from where we were living, I went to hang out and listen to the music. It was more difficult and depressing than I had expected. I felt irritated that I couldn't grab a drink the way I had always done in the past. I felt alone and even undesirable because I was not participating in the normal drinking behavior of a bar patron.

Instead of leaving the bar or ordering a beer, I came up with a creative thought that helped me change my focus from wanting a drink. I began to think about being in the bar with all of my good friends and family. I imagined they were all there to celebrate me, some of them having driven hours just to be there. That changed the situation. I told myself that if there was a celebration going on in that smoky little bar that was for me, then my mood would be very different. The heavy burden I was feeling, sitting alone with my feet kicked up on a chair and no drink in my hand, would not be there. I realized it wasn't the bar I was struggling with. It was my own feelings.

Using my imagination in that way helped me recognize my mood is dependent on my *thoughts* and not entirely on my circumstances. Of course, I don't suggest hanging out in smoky bars when you are trying to live a healthier lifestyle. I am showing you how the power of thinking can help you through some difficult situations.

Another example of the power of working with my thoughts was at Christmastime just two years after I quit drinking. We had our family visiting, and someone brought an expensive bottle of scotch to be shared. I brought out my fancy antique glasses for everyone to use and let them go at it.

Sitting on the floor in the living room, watching everyone enjoy the aged scotch, I inhaled that powerful, familiar scent and began to think, "Now why is it that I'm not letting myself drink when other people get to?" I looked down and noticed my dog and cat were both curled up sleeping next to me, and I was reminded that not all living creatures drink alcohol. That may sound silly, but it helped me to break the train of thought that was making it very difficult for me to be comfortable with my choice not to drink.

The thought of my animals led me to think about the millions and millions of people on the planet who don't use alcohol in their lives and actually never have. It reminded me that the destructive way I had lived in the past is not the only way for people to live. In fact, most people do not live the way I did—intoxicating themselves whenever they can.

These are just a few of the ways that I worked with my thoughts during troubling times. I encourage you to ask other people what they did during their difficult moments and how they coached themselves through them. And you don't need to limit that to people who have quit using drugs and alcohol, though they are a good source. Look also to people who have accomplished any significant goal or feat. Read about a mountain climber and what he said to himself when the wind was blistering cold and he felt he had no strength to go on. Find out what thoughts he used to continue on. Look at what successful people have done to help themselves and see if you can apply some of their techniques to your own life.

This is a time of transition, and however long it takes, you need to nurture yourself through the experience. If you feel that it will help you for the moment to stay in bed, then stay in bed. If you have friends who will hang out with you, then call them. But whatever you do, do not be harsh with yourself as you are healing. The psychological process of healing works the same way as the physical process—if you continually pick at a wound, it won't heal. So don't pick on yourself while you are getting better.

⌘

Chapter 16

PASSION

"If you want to build a ship,
don't drum up the people to gather wood,
divide the work, and give orders.
Instead, teach them to yearn
of the vast and endless sea."

Antoine de Saint Exupery

While observing my thoughts, feelings and behaviors as I went through the difficult process of releasing my addictions, I came to understand and accept that passion, like desire, can be misunderstood and distorted. However, I also now know that allowing ourselves to experience passion fully is another key to sustained health and enjoyment in our lives.

Because allowing ourselves to feel and express passion can be extremely beneficial when healing from an addiction, passion needs to be encouraged and enjoyed as we recuperate. However, in order to experience passion in a beneficial way, we need to be able to separate it from distorted desires.

In the past when I thought, *"I have to drink, I have to smoke, I have to take drugs,"* I would go through great difficulties to make sure I got whatever I wanted. That usually meant ignoring my basic needs for nutrition and rest. If I was very "passionate" about getting a particular substance for myself, I could rarely be stopped until I got it.

In those instances my "passion" was not serving me at all. In fact, this is a perfect example of a distorted desire masquerading as an authentic passion response. It was not an energy of love and creativity that was stimulating my enthusiasm and desire. It was my *fear*. It was my fear that no activity could satisfy me in the way that those old habits could. It was my fear of feeling empty and miserable that led me to constantly rush out and find something to numb myself with as soon as possible.

I also came to realize that I had a great fear that I could never feel joy, satisfaction or fun in my life without my old familiar habits of using alcohol or another substance to make me feel good. That fear was so strong that I nearly lost my life because of it—more than once.

The longer a person has been using drugs and alcohol, the more unbelievable is the thought that life can be fun, fulfilling and joyful without substances. The further we get from experiencing joy in our lives without the use of drugs or alcohol, the more impossible it seems that we can attain joy in a natural way.

For someone like me, who had been primarily cut off from naturally generated good feelings for so long, accepting that life can be enjoyable and satisfying without the use of a substance was a difficult thing to do. But I have found a way to make it easier.

First, remind yourself to be patient. Tell yourself that good feelings *will* eventually return to you. Then *allow* yourself to experience your authentic passion as often as you can in the present. Allowing yourself to experience authentic passion means that when you have a simple pleasant experience—a laugh, a smile, or a giggle—you do not diminish it. You don't let your old habit of cynicism reduce the value of that experience. It can be difficult to try to convince yourself that you can be passionate about your life in the future when you are feeling so terrible in the present. So rather than forcing yourself to simply *think* that it can be done, the key is to allow yourself to experience the bits of passion that you already have. I say "allow" because for someone stuck in the habit of feeling terrible, allowing a positive experience usually has to come before you can create a positive experience. That's how it was for me. I was very stuck in feeling bad, and I had to give myself permission to enjoy *anything*—even the slightest thing.

Learning to allow yourself to experience passion means that when you feel excited—or even slightly interested—about a new, healthy idea, you're willing try it out. So allow yourself to feel the goodness and excitement of new ideas. You might change your mind about their worth later, but when you have an opportunity to feel good or excited about a positive thing—seize it!

By allowing yourself to experience any naturally occurring good feelings without feeling unworthy or foolish for it, you are building on an important ability that can eventually lead you to experience deep feelings of passion about life. Those positive experiences can benefit you greatly in your healing.

Of course, as with everything in the process of overcoming addictions, you will find that drawing upon your capacity for *patience* will be an extremely valuable practice. Being patient will serve you in everything you do in your healing process.

For the greater portion of my life, no matter how I tried, I always ended up feeling that my life was flat and empty. In spite of occasionally experiencing circumstances that many people would envy, such as money, interesting lovers, and travel to beautiful places in the world, I felt no joy. To me, my life was flat and joyless, so I drank, thinking I was filling it. I could not appreciate the things that I had because I was tormented by my strong negative feelings. I always felt bad unless I was drinking.

After so many years of using substances to numb myself to *all of life*, including my authentic passions, I was unable to experience joy in my normal day-to-day activities. I was attempting to get some joy through my addictions, and on occasion it helped somewhat, but mostly my addictions only temporarily numbed my bad feelings. I later realized that by numbing my negative feelings, I had also diminished my positive feelings about life—the authentic joyful feelings.

I now know that we cannot numb our bad feelings without squeezing out some of the good as well. Although doctors attempt to help us deal with our bad feelings by numbing them with medications, if you ask people who have taken antidepressant drugs, they will tell you that among some of the disadvantages is that the intensity of certain pleasures is diminished.

Some of us were taught that passion is self-indulgent, or even bad. As a result, passion tends to be dismissed as insignificant and even problematic. However, based on my own experience, I know that passion can be a great support for a person who is attempting to overcome an addictive habit. That is why it's so important to cultivate passionate feelings for something other than a drink or a drug.

Allow your passion to help you to heal.

⌘

Chapter 17

MEMORIES

"It was the best of times,
it was the worst of times;
it was the age of wisdom,
it was the age of foolishness."

Charles Dickens

Recently, after I had stopped drinking and smoking, I was driving around Los Angeles. I passed a location by the beach where I had spent a lot of time partying as a teenager. I immediately began to reminisce about the late-night beer drinking, pot smoking bonfires, and *usually* fun-filled nights that my friends and I used to have there. As soon as I began thinking about those times, I started to feel sad and even lonely as I longed for the good times. Suddenly I had an extreme desire for beer and cigarettes, just like I did in the old days.

Later that day I went to a nearby market where, in my twenties, I used to buy alcohol—a *lot* of alcohol. As I walked through the aisles, I felt sadly let down. I remembered the contented feeling I used to have as I filled up my shopping cart almost daily with ample supplies of vodka, wine and beer while preparing for my leisurely evening of doing nothing but hanging out, drinking and smoking.

But then it hit me. It is true that there were some fun times in my past that included drinking. And it is true that having my drinks and cigarettes to keep me company was, more often than not, consistently comforting. But as my memories continued to return, I realized there was a lot more to my inebriated past than just those "fun" times.

I thought about a guy I had met many years ago while partying with my friends at the very same beach spot I had driven past earlier in the day. I was fifteen years old then, and he was in his mid-twenties. I had agreed to hang out with him the following evening.

When I got together with the guy the next night, we drove to that same spot on the beach and sat and drank and smoked for a while. Suddenly he got aggressive and mean and grabbed me.

It was really bad. I didn't want him touching me, much less having sex with me, but he forced me anyway. The entire time he was at it, he was completely insensitive about the sand and he was hurting me. He continued to do so for the rest of the night and on into the light of the next morning.

Looking back I now know that was rape. But at the time, as a young teenager, I was so unsure of my rights as a human being and so lacking an understanding of my inherent worth, that I did not realize I had the right to refuse—and I definitely did not have the physical strength to protect myself against him.

At that time I was so disturbed by the whole incident that normally I would have told someone. However, because I did not want anything to limit my partying lifestyle by having restrictions enforced upon me, because I was afraid of upsetting my family, and because I was afraid that guy might come back to kill me if I told on him, I kept the incident to myself. In fact, I kept many such incidents to myself, continuing to suffer the humiliation and danger that often goes along with constant inebriation.

So while it is tempting for those of us who are healing addictions to reflect on some of the pleasures of the past with nostalgia, it's important to remember *all* of the facts—not just the pleasant ones. However, it's not beneficial to remember everything to the point where you feel bad, stupid, or worthless—definitely not that.

The reason that it's important for you to remember *all sides* of your intoxication in the past is so you can feel better in the present. Even though you can use humiliating and frightening memories to keep yourself in line with your goal of better health, try not to use those memories as a reason to negatively judge yourself as a person. Instead, try to use your negative memories as a guideline to help you remember where you do *not* want to go in the present, as well as to motivate you to think about where you *do* want to go in the future.

It's possible that when you pass an outdoor barbeque on a warm summer day, the smells of food and the sounds of laughter will stir up good memories of drinking beer and hanging out with friends. If you were struggling with addiction during the time of those "good memories," even though you had those moments of pleasure, it's important to remember the turmoil that occurred during those times as well.

I cannot count the number of alcohol blackouts I have had in my life. It's possible I had more nights with them than without them. The frightening thought is that I don't know what occurred during many of those blackouts. But what's even more frightening to me are the partial flashes of the terrible things I do remember that happened while I was deeply intoxicated. Let me just say that I'm glad cell phones with video capability were not around then. And worse than the humiliation and embarrassment I recall in those partial memories were the numerous physically dangerous situations I was in because I was intoxicated.

Yes, it was sad for me to realize that the "fun" times in my past were over, but it was even more sad to realize that I had given up the greater part of my life to alcohol and drugs. For over twenty years my daily life—not to mention my body—was lost in alcohol, drugs, eating disorders, rehabs, hospitals, psychiatrists, psychologists, antidepressant drugs, misery, despair, and very often, demeaning sex.

I remember when I was a child, I enjoyed myself in much more creative ways—through art, song, dance, sports, and, when I was very young, math. I imagine those were my true interests and desires. They were the desires I had before I was distorted by my deeply despairing feelings through long periods of depression.

But today, even with so many years lost in misery, shame and depression—*all is not lost*. I can still choose to act on my original desires for creativity and goodness by expressing the creative abilities I had enjoyed as a child. Those abilities did not disappear.

When I am saddened by a memory, I now know that I have choices. I could choose to spend my time in deep regret about my troubling past. But if I want to feel bad, then why not resort to my old behavior and watch my body deteriorate as I slip back into the misery of having to drink myself unconscious every night. I don't want that. And that is my point—deep down we all want to feel better and be free and healthy.

It does not serve us to dwell too much on memories of our terrible past. It would help us more to remember that *all is not lost*. Today, and in any day, we can begin to create new, interesting, and fulfilling experiences. As a matter of fact, if I want to avoid going back to alcohol and drugs, I *must* create new, interesting, and fulfilling experiences.

Once again, if you find yourself grieving over old times as you sort through your memories of the past, it's important to remind yourself that *all is not lost*—in fact, much has been *gained*. It takes a great deal of strength and courage to survive some of the intense turmoil that goes along with a life of addiction. When you choose to give up the substances, you get to keep all of the strength and courage you gained. That is yours to keep. And it is that very strength and courage you have gained in your struggle with your addiction that will help you to create new, more fulfilling experiences in your life without the use of substances. All is not lost.

If you find yourself reminiscing about the pleasure of using substances in the past—missing that, wanting a drink or a drug—remember that those memories are only a fragment of your story. You know that if it was all as perfect as we want to remember it, not only would we still be doing it, but so would everyone else.

⌘

Chapter 18

BREAKDOWN

*"The deeper that sorrow carves into your being
the more joy you can contain.
Is not the cup that holds your wine the very cup
that was burned in the potter's oven?"*

Kahlil Gibran

A few years ago I found myself lying in a bed in the emergency room of a hospital, held down by leather restraints on my arms and legs. Earlier that night I had taken some anti-anxiety medication prescribed by my doctor, along with a lot of wine and vodka. Even though I had been in a blackout, I had somehow managed to reach the suicide hotline, and they sent the paramedics, who then took me to the emergency room.

From the emergency room, with me still in restraints, they pushed my bed into a small room

149

and stationed a uniformed policeman at the door. I cannot remember why they did that. I suppose I had done something bad to have a policeman guarding me, but I don't remember what it was. All I remember is that when I came out of my blackout, I was in the hospital and not in my apartment or jail.

They made me drink charcoal that night to absorb the pills and alcohol in my stomach—which was, of course, disgusting. Even worse than that was when I had to use the bathroom. Since I had consumed massive amounts of alcohol that night, I had to go quite a lot. But because I was in restraints, I had to use a bedpan. That was not the worst part. Since my hands were tied up, I was forced to ask someone to bring me the bed pan—and take it away—every time I had to go. I don't remember if I was more angry or more embarrassed about that, but I do remember feeling extremely bothered about having a policeman lingering around my door.

The next day when I woke up, I was in a different hospital room—one that I do not remember entering—and my restraints were gone. My head felt heavy, and I had no idea what I was doing there.

After a while, a handsome young doctor

walked in and asked me if I remembered him. Mildly embarrassed, I shook my head no. He explained that he was the ER doctor from the night before. He said that I had called him some pretty nasty names.

Then I remembered the restraints they had put on me, and I thought to myself, "Well, that would make sense, me being nasty—putting me in restraints and all." I did not even want to think about what I might have done that was the cause for the restraints. I could not remember much before 10:00 p.m. the previous night, and dreading to hear the horrible details, I could not bring myself to ask what had happened.

I told the doctor I was sorry I had been so rude to him. He was kind but brief in his response, and he quickly left the room. I sat on the bed for a while in my hospital gown, just sort of moaning to myself about what a horrible, hopeless wreck I was.

Then an older and very stern-looking white-coated man walked into my room. He was the psychiatric doctor on the unit, but he behaved more like a high school vice-principal. He shook his head at me and told me in doctor lingo to cut out the crap, get off my butt, and not to let him see me in there again.

Even though he was kind of harsh, I appreciated what he was saying. He was not telling me to take psychiatric drugs or asking me about my childhood. He seemed to be saying that I was not messed up in the head, only stupid and irresponsible.

I actually appreciated that. He seemed to be saying that I was really okay, unlike the other doctors who had always implied I was doomed to failure without their expertise and medications. Although he told me not to come back, I could not leave then because I was on a seventy-two-hour hold.

After the doctor left, I walked to the nurse's station to see about a desperately needed cigarette. Thankfully, I had some in my personal belongings from when they had admitted me the night before, and the nurse gave me one. I mentally patted myself on the back in appreciation. I may have been a suicidal drunk, but I had made certain that I had my smokes—good girl.

I walked down the hall to a tiny atrium area, where we were permitted to smoke. Before I went in I looked warily through the glass walls and saw another patient standing, staring, and smoking. I determined that she (or he—I really could not tell) seemed safe enough, so I went in, and together we smoked our cigarettes in silence.

As we smoked, I began to feel trapped, and I had the desperate thought, "Oh my God—I have to get out here. I really have to get out of here." Then I remembered that I was not in there voluntarily. They had me on the seventy-two-hour hold. That is when I started to panic.

Feeling claustrophobic, I put out my cigarette and rushed straight to the patient pay phone that was hanging on the wall in the hallway. Feeling so ashamed of myself for ending up there in the first place, I just wanted to get back to my apartment, where this terrible episode had started. I did not want to go through the whole program of doctors, and medications, and confinement—again.

As I was placing my call, I remembered the last time that I was on a seventy-two-hour hold. At that time it was actually a welcome escape to be able to zone out for a couple of days. This time, however, I felt a horrific wave of suffocating doom engulfing me. I desperately needed to get out of there.

The person I called was my ex-husband. He was a criminal defense attorney, and I hoped he could do something to get me released. Thankfully, he called a mutual friend (who was also an attorney), who came to the hospital to see me.

Even though he was not a relative, he somehow managed to set me free. I don't know what he did, but right after he left I found myself outside the hospital, waiting for a taxi to go home.

I returned to my apartment, where I discovered the aftermath of the night before in the mess of bottles lying around the room. There had been policemen and firemen in my tiny apartment, and for all I know, probably some of my neighbors too. Although the previous night was mostly a blur to me, I knew it had to have been quite a scene. As I looked around at my rumpled bed and the trashed room where it had all taken place, a horrible sinking feeling washed over me.

If you have ever spent an evening in an alcoholic blackout, you can understand some of the feelings that I had as I looked around at the "scene of the crime." I felt shame, disgust, fear, and a great desire to make it all go away. But I could not. Standing there totally alone, all I knew to do was to get back to my usual routine, which consisted of trying to find something to do to keep myself occupied, trying to earn some money to support myself, and of course, trying not to get into too much trouble as I returned to my habit of drinking. And that night, to calm myself, and also to escape my shame, I again drank myself to sleep.

That was the end of that breakdown, but it was not to be my last. For some people a breakdown will motivate them to stop their self-destructive behavior. For others like myself, who have had many breakdowns, it is not always enough.

It's different for everyone, but for me, I felt strongly that deep down I was as shameful and bad as all of my negative behaviors. I had been in so many awful situations throughout my life, and I had suffered so deeply from my intense negative feelings about myself, that I truly believed I was a bad person. So I felt, "What's the use? I'm so bad. There's no hope for me to be better, so I might as well keep drinking."

If you suffer in the same way I did—from the belief that you are a bad person because of the many bad experiences that you have had—I hope you will reconsider that judgment. What I learned day after day, after I stopped drinking and taking drugs, is that it is vital to remember your true inner goodness and worth as a person. If you do not, you will continue to believe that you are terrible, and that belief will make it much more difficult for you to make positive changes in your life.

You must teach yourself that you are not a terrible person just because you have been through terrible times. You are not your experiences.

You need to notice how you treat yourself day after day. Learning to treat yourself well is the building block of your new health. You must learn to shower yourself with kindness.

The best thing you can do for yourself as you struggle to give up an addictive habit and become healthy is to learn to feel you are worthwhile and good. And you need to practice feeling that toward yourself as often as you can.

⌘

Chapter 19

BODY

*"Our own physical body possesses a wisdom
which we who inhabit the body lack.
We give it orders which make no sense."*

Henry Miller

I remember when I first quit drinking, taking drugs, and smoking, I was easily encouraged or discouraged when I would read about the different general time frames that were given for physical recovery after various forms of substance abuse. So for me, it became important to remind myself that although there are some general ideas about how long it will take for a physical body to recover, there are differences in the amount of abuse each of us has endured and differences in the strength and tolerance of each of our bodies.

I noticed that when I compared my physical

recovery process to what I had read was the expected period of time for recovery, I began to criticize myself and my body because my body seemed to be taking much longer than the average time to heal. However, because I had learned that such criticism is an obstruction to healing and overcoming addictions, I had to stop comparing myself. I had to realize that I was not *bad* because I had a longer way to go in my recovery than many people. I also came to realize that because of the extreme strain I had placed on my body for so many years, I required even *more* TLC—tender, loving care—than some.

There were many days during the early stages of my healing that my body was so weak, I didn't think I could get out of bed. It was frustrating to feel so weak, particularly because when I was drinking, I had a great deal of energy. Drinking had stimulated me. Because I desperately wanted to feel energetic again, it was a great temptation for me to drink

However, I have learned that no matter how difficult it is to resist a temptation, it is possible to do it. It's also important to congratulate yourself when you do resist a temptation so you don't experience the entire process of giving up an addiction as deprivation. Give yourself credit when you deserve it.

When I felt the intense overwhelming urge to energize my body with alcohol, I was able to resist by reminding myself of all that my body had suffered already. I knew it was severely abused, nearly in shock, and absolutely needed me to leave it alone and not put any more toxins into it. I needed to make healthy choices so that my body could return to health, as bodies naturally try to do.

What many recovering addicts do not realize is that when their body is depleted and malnourished, as the bodies of so many substance abusers are, their emotional state can be dramatically affected. When I was seventeen I was hospitalized for anorexia. Fortunately, since I was modeling at that time, my work was not so physically demanding. I simply needed to pose for the camera. I would have been unable to do much more because I was always exhausted from lack of nutrition.

In that weakened state, it was extremely difficult for me to process information that required critical thinking. Also, I could not deal with even the smallest emotional difficulty or negative feelings without responding irrationally, if I responded at all. I tell you this because, having experienced malnutrition so severely in my past, I was able to recognize its signs when I quit drinking.

Soon after I quit modeling and began putting on some necessary weight, I often substituted alcohol for meals. This went on for years. I did not take vitamins on any consistent basis, as I probably should have. And although I was at a healthy weight when I finally quit drinking many years later, I was malnourished from so many years of mistreating my body.

This kind of stress on the body is important to recognize if you have been a heavy drinker or have used drugs for a long period of time. As I can tell you from my many periods of physical depletion, your moods, your thoughts, and your decisions can be negatively influenced in a powerful way when your body is weak and undernourished. Therefore, when you have strong negative feelings, you might mistakenly believe that you are in a bad emotional state because of personal problems, when actually it might be that you are feeling bad because your body is in a state of depletion. You then run the risk of choosing to drink again or use drugs to overcome that negative mood. It really is important to know that a depressed body can depress your mood.

When I saw the doctor at the beginning of my

last detox, he tested my blood for deficiencies. I believe, based on how sick I felt and how long and heavily only I knew I had abused substances, the damage was far worse than a mere blood test could show. However, the test did show a deficiency in the B vitamins and a few other areas. So in an effort to take better care of my body, I started taking vitamins and nutritional supplements.

Although I still think that was a wise choice for my body, taking supplements did not miraculously make me feel better. So I began to research nutrition on my own. I studied the cycles of toxins in our bodies, the organs they tax, and the cleansing processes our bodies go through. If you are interested, it's easy enough to do your own research. However, from my own extensive research, I can tell you that a good basic starting point for health would be plenty of fresh fruits, fresh vegetables, light proteins, and fresh water. Learn for yourself what is best for your body. See your doctor, ask a nutritionist, read up on ways to stay healthy. And, remember that it is very important to rest when you need it.

Depending on the severity of your abuse and the constitution of your body, you may also need a great deal of *patience* in bringing your body to health. I know I did. Keep in mind that the body is often slower to recover than the psyche. However, when given the opportunity, the body has an amazing innate capacity to heal itself.

For understanding the health of your brain, it's helpful to know that there is a process called "neuro-plasticity." That is the ability of the brain to reorganize healthy neurons and to create a *new* information circuit. This means that we are not doomed. We can think clearly again! I noticed a significant improvement in my memory after about six months (remember what I said earlier, no comparing). In time, my memory got even better—naturally. As Joe Dispenza, author of *Evolve Your Brain: The Science of Changing Your Mind,* says:

> . . . *research is beginning to verify that the brain is not as hardwired as we once thought. We now know that any of us, at any age, can gain new knowledge, process it in the brain, and formulate new thoughts, and that this process will formulate new footprints in the brain—that is, new synaptic connections develop.*

So as you leave your addictions behind, if you find yourself feeling weak and forgetful at times, remember to be extra patient with yourself as you wait for your body to recover.

While you do that, remember also to focus on

being the best possible caretaker of your body that you can be. No matter how depleted your body might have been in the past or what state your body is currently in, treat yourself kindly, healthfully, and without judgment.

⌘

Chapter 20

ᏉNSOMNIA

"When I woke up this morning
my girlfriend asked me, 'Did you sleep well?'
I said, 'No, I made a few mistakes.'"

Steven Wright

I had my first alcoholic blackout when I was thirteen years old, but it was not until my early twenties that I used alcohol on a nightly basis to purposely black out so I could sleep at night. I have had trouble sleeping since I was about ten. My extreme sadness and constant flow of tears kept me awake nightly. Lying in bed late at night and thinking about other people in the world who were sound asleep was disturbing to me. Thinking about that made me feel even more desperate about not sleeping because I felt that I *should* be sleeping.

When I was fifteen I discovered "The Late Show" with David Letterman. That was significant for me because not only did I realize that the entire living world around me was not asleep late at night, which was a huge thing in itself, but also that someone could make me—a suicidal, insomniac teenager—crack a smile. That was quite an accomplishment for a guy who didn't even have to buy me a drink.

However, later in my adult life, my fear of being awake when everyone else was sleeping had become so troubling for me that I came to absolutely depend on alcohol for sleep. That is how I coped with my fear of not being able to go to sleep.

As soon as I made it to the morning, I would smoke a cigarette and busy myself with things to do and places to go to distract me from my fear. If I felt panicky or alone, I would jump in my car and drive—anywhere. If there was nothing to do, then I might start my day with a beer or a Bloody Mary.

If I felt bored while I was waiting someplace, I would smoke to pass the time. If I felt bored where I could not smoke, then I would anxiously count the minutes until I could grab a cigarette and a strong drink to calm my nerves.

In the late afternoon and into the evening, I would drink heavily until eventually I'd reach my goal of passing out—hopefully in my own bed. I justified all of this behavior by telling myself that at least in this way, I didn't have to feel so worried about the inevitable, dreaded nighttime.

Later in my life, when I was prescribed anti-anxiety pills in lieu of drinking and I still couldn't sleep, I noticed something. As I lay awake in bed, watching VH1's "Insomniac Music Theater," I noticed that I was actually enjoying my time alone doing nothing. I knew that my initial relaxation was from the drugs, but even so, it showed me that it was *my negative thoughts and feelings about not sleeping* that were the problem—not the fact that I was awake. There were no sleep police. No one cared if I was awake but me. In fact, many television programmers counted on me, and people like me, to be awake at such a late (or early) hour.

Now that I am able to relax without alcohol or medication, I have found that I can really enjoy being awake late at night. It can be very private and peaceful, and I enjoy the fact that time seems to slow down. That makes it easier for me to feel that I can truly relax.

This is an amazing turnaround from the little girl who cried all through the night, and from the adult woman who drank herself unconscious for years to survive the fear of being awake late at night. That remarkable change occurred when I was finally able to absorb the fact that it was *okay* for me to be awake, and that if I wanted to, I could even appreciate and enjoy the calm, private time of the late night and early morning.

Before I quit drinking I feared the thought of not having alcohol to put me to sleep. I knew I could get at least one round of sleeping pills from my doctor, but when they were gone, then what? I would still have the fear of the night, and as I have discovered over the years, the longer I avoid a fear, the larger it becomes. In addition to that, I was also trying very hard to revive my body, not depress it. So adding drugs to go to sleep at night was not a good option for me. Instead, I chose to brave my dread of the nights in a sober state.

As it turned out, after my initial physical withdrawal the first week or so, learning to over-come my fear and appreciate the nighttime was not as hard to do as I expected. In fact, now that I have learned to enjoy the night, there are even moments when I am slightly disappointed when I see the early morning sunlight creeping through my window.

It's not that I never sleep—I do. But it's that I

no longer have the fears associated with going to sleep that I used to have. That is because I learned that if there are times when I cannot sleep, not only is there nothing to fear, but there might even be something to look forward to—especially on TV.

Another thing that changed for me when I quit dousing myself with alcohol every day, flooding myself with cigarette smoke, and depriving myself of basic nutritional needs, was that my nerves naturally calmed down on their own. That made it a lot easier for me to be able to sit still, to live through my fear about the nighttime, and to have a much more peaceful rest than when I had alcohol running through my system.

If you can learn not to fear the lonely late-night hours, then you can eventually learn to love those hours. The main thing is to learn not to worry so much about your sleep patterns. People sleep at all hours. People go through different phases and cycles of sleep. If your lifestyle allows you to sleep until two-o-clock in the afternoon and you do—so what.

During the initial stages of quitting a substance, you need to let yourself and your body adjust and reset itself naturally, without force. Also, remember that as you eliminate disturbing fears—just as when you eliminate the substances—your body will regain its more natural cycles and rhythms. Therefore, if you have some different or unusual sleep or non-sleep patterns, you don't need to feel that something is wrong.

For me, the problem with being awake at night came from my thoughts, beliefs, and feelings about it, not the actual being awake. The more I've been able to experience being awake in the middle of the night with this new understanding, the more enjoyable the night has become.

⌘

Chapter 21

❡DENTITY

"The Beatles exist apart from my Self.
I am not really Beatle George.
Beatle George is like a suit or shirt
that I once wore on occasion,
and until the end of my life,
people may see that shirt and mistake it for me."

George Harrison

When I first quit drinking, I no longer had a clear sense of who I was as a person. I felt as if I had lost my identity. I felt I was no longer myself as I had known me in the past. If I was no longer the heavy-drinking party girl, then who was I?

Since I no longer had the identity of a party girl, I was left feeling so self-conscious and clumsy that simply walking from one side of a room to the other was an embarrassing task. That insecurity made me even more nervous about changing my habits because I felt that if I could not behave like a "normal" person, then I was really going to have trouble letting go of my addictions.

Looking back now with much more understanding, I can see how natural those insecure feelings were. I had abruptly gone from one extreme of being completely inebriated to the other extreme of being completely not inebriated. Although I was not aware of it at the time, it's normal for a person to feel uncomfortable while transitioning from one state of being to another.

As you go forward to put your addictions behind you, it can take some time to get comfortable in your "new skin." But it will eventually happen. The more time that goes by, the more comfortable you will be without your old habits.

Recently I had a day filled with shame and remorse as I remembered many terrible things in my past. That night I had a great dream. I dreamt I was trying to remove a photo from my computer screen. As I was figuring out how to do that, I looked closely at the picture and began to study it. In the foreground I saw my dog sleeping on a long couch, and leaning against the couch was an acoustic guitar. Yet, as I looked beyond the couch in the picture, I realized that this was my mother's home from when I was a child. At the time she lived in that home, I did not, and I was deeply troubled by heart-wrenching feelings of abandonment.

As I continued to look at the picture in the dream, suddenly I was *in* the picture! I was no longer looking at the picture from the outside, but I was inside the picture, and I was able to go on to explore the next room that I could see through an open door.

As I walked into that room—an informal dining room full of gorgeous, tall, white lilies in vases—I realized in the dream that because the time in my life that this house represented was so deeply traumatizing for me, I needed to stir up feelings of despair. So in my dream I purposely began to do so. I began to groan and cry.

But as I moved on through the rest of the house, I realized that this was not my *mother's* house. This was *my* house. And it was a *great* house! I ceased my despair then, and I felt awe and excitement as I looked around the rooms and saw that everything in them was perfect for me. I saw many unique details that thrilled me, such as the unusually high ceilings with black cherry wood crown molding around the top. I saw a wonderful little yard with green grass and two beautiful chaise lounges for lazing outdoors.

After exploring a bit more, I woke up to find my dog sitting at the side of my bed. I figured that I must have been so excited that I was actually crying out loud and woke him up.

Although this dream was personal to me, what it demonstrates can be applied to anyone. As people who have struggled deeply with alcohol or drugs, we have all had difficult periods in our lives. Those periods would be symbolized in the dream as the *construction* phase of the house—the construction phase of our lives. That construction period is a messy time, when everything is in chaos. When we end construction—when we quit drinking or using drugs—we can choose to move into that great house, or we can continue to view it as the clutter of a construction zone that it *was*. We can choose to call our finished house a messy construction site and visualize all the paint, the workmen and the mess, or we can see the house for what it is—a wonderful dwelling that we can enjoy living in today.

Our past traumas and our struggles with drinking and drugging can be viewed as part of the construction mess that went into building our present lives. It's now up to each of us how we think of our lives *today*. Do we continue to live in the disarray of the construction zone of our past, or do we live in the magnificent home of our present.

In my experience, letting go of my old habits and becoming a person who lived "straight" turned out to be less of a challenge than I had anticipated. I discovered that the problem of *identity* was only as huge as I made it, and the extent of the problem depended solely on how much I chose to focus on feeling lost because I was not drinking, using drugs, or smoking. I learned to notice when I felt uncomfortable not doing those things, and drawing on my newly discovered inner strength, I taught myself to ignore that feeling. The uncomfortable feeling would always pass, and I would return to feeling glad that I did not give in to my old desires and make myself sick again.

Some people worry that when they quit drinking or using drugs, they will become a "born-again addict" and begin preaching to others about the error of their ways. That is a choice you can make. You can become anything you want. You can become that, or you can become a "new homeowner"—or anything else that you choose.

When you stop using substances, you are presented with the opportunity to see who you are behind all of your old, unhealthy behaviors. It's your choice what, if any, label you take on for yourself. You do not need to fear becoming someone you are not. Instead, you can use your newfound status of "not-knowing-who-you-are-anymore" as the ultimate opportunity to become more of who you *truly* are—your real self. You will be able to discover the wonderful person you have always been behind the negative behaviors that you are now abandoning. You can learn how to allow your true self to shine outward as you choose what can be a most amazing and gratifying path of healthy and joyful living.

⌘

Chapter 22

TEMPTATION

*"I count him braver who overcomes his desires
than him who conquers his enemies;
for the hardest victory is the victory over self."*

Aristotle

Soon after I quit drinking and had started on my way to better health, I went to a big family gathering for Christmas in California. My mother, brother, sister, nieces, nephews and many other members of my extended family were all there at my mother's house in Los Angeles.

This was only a few weeks after my terrifying breakdown when I found myself crouched on my living room floor, suffering from the DT's and having horrible panic attacks. Because that was so frightening, I had not had a single drink of alcohol since then and was not worried about being tempted by the wine and spirits that were certain to be at the gathering. I felt really strong because I had a determination that I had never had before. I was committed to getting to the bottom of this whole problem of addiction because, frankly, I was just plain sick of dealing with it. I had been a slave to my overwhelming desire for alcohol and other substances for too long, and I was now on a mission to get through the difficulties of not drinking in order to discover, if possible, the pleasures of living a healthier life.

So, as I approached the first Christmas of my adult life without drinking, it was not as though I felt like a superhero who was able to resist all temptation. It was more that I just didn't *think* I would have a desire for any alcohol.

Oh, how wrong I was!

The sweet smell of the wine, the familiar whoosh of a beer can being popped open, the dazzling bubbles in the champagne, the promising clank of ice in a glass of tonic—everything amid the warmth and laughter of family and friends—all of that was *very* enticing, indeed.

I was truly caught by surprise. When I was at home before my trip to see the family, I had felt so determined and so certain I would not be tempted that I did not even consider libations as I made my holiday plans. But it was on that trip that I learned what everyone who is new to sobriety must learn—temptation is going to be a part of the game of giving up alcohol *no matter how determined you may be*. That Christmas I was loaded with determination, but during the party the temptation to drink was so strong that I felt as if I had no will at all.

It's important to understand that no matter how strong your resolve may be, there will be times of powerful temptation, and you may have an almost overwhelming desire to return to your old habit of using drugs or alcohol. Temptation is generally at its most powerful when a person first gives up an addictive habit. Given that, I found my experience of strong temptation became more tolerable when I reminded myself that temptation is completely normal—*and even acceptable*.

Once I understood the "normality" of experiencing strong temptations, especially after the long-term substance abuse I had, then the temptations began to lose the power over me that I *believed* they had. The more I was able to simply live through my intense desires for alcohol or other substances and accept the accompanying feelings of anxiety as a *temporary* part of my healing process, the less I was tempted to act on my desires to use substances.

Before I left home to go to my mother's house for that Christmas party, I had talked to my physician. He pointed out that there would surely be champagne and other spirits available at the party, and he suggested that I think about those drinks as "poison" that everyone would be ingesting. He told me to think about how great I would be for not taking poison.

When my physician suggested that, I had to laugh to myself. He was essentially telling me to sit around during my holiday *celebration* and spend my time judging everyone while thinking about their looming demise from the poison they were drinking. I said nothing to him, but I knew that what he was telling me was not the advice I needed. I knew that in order not to give in to my desire to drink during the upcoming party, I would need to pay attention to my *own* experience and try to understand what was going on with *me*—not what was going on with everyone else.

I was very familiar with the pleasures of drinking, so criticizing other people for enjoying those pleasures did not make any sense to me. And it would not help me control my desire to drink. I knew that there had to be another way to understand and deal with temptation during the party.

As temptation unexpectedly attacked me

during that Christmas party, and on through the holiday period, I decided that rather than sitting there helplessly trapped in the silent agony of my powerful desire to drink, I would pay attention to my thoughts and feelings *about* desiring alcohol as I was experiencing them.

Observing your thoughts is a useful thing to do anytime you are struggling, but especially when you are tempted to drink or use drugs again. *When you feel that strong desire to drink or use drugs, you can step back and study your thoughts and feelings as if you were a loving friend to yourself.* Rather than allowing the desire to overpower you and force you to return to your addictive habits, you can learn to redirect your attention by focusing on your thoughts *about* the desire that you are experiencing.

As I did that during the Christmas holidays, I noticed thoughts crossing my mind like, "If Mom didn't know about my terrible withdrawal experience, then maybe I would have a drink." Or, "If I hadn't *promised* myself not to drink, then maybe it would be alright to have some wine." Or, "Hmmm, no one really has to know." Paying attention to those thoughts and then exploring why I might be thinking them became the focus of my attention rather than focusing on my powerful desire to have a drink. By doing that I was able to let the strong feeling of desire continue to happen inside me, but I did not respond with my old habit of giving into it. Instead, I allowed the desire to flow through me without acting on it.

What I was actually doing was accepting temptation as a normal part of being human. It's particularly "normal" for someone who has suffered through addictions.

If you have this understanding, then you can learn to let temptation run its course. First, you feel and accept your intense desire for substances as you experience that desire. Then, you practice turning your attention away from the desire and you learn how to let it simply flow through you without acting on it. You will discover that even an overwhelming need for addictive substances will eventually pass. It always does.

It helped me a lot to be curious about what was *really going on* behind my strong desire to use substances. For example, I would ask myself, "What is the *feeling* that I am trying to achieve by getting drunk?" Though we may not all have the same response, what I found in answer to that question was that I was seeking a feeling of *comfort, contentment* and *well-being*. I realized that I was not simply trying to feel high. Yes, I sought excitement and happiness, but I discovered that what I *really* wanted was to feel safe, and to feel a loving connection to the people around me. So on the deepest level, what I was seeking from alcohol was an *internal experience of well-being and connectedness.*

So with that in mind, I realized that my method of using substances to try to achieve an experience of well-being and connectedness was actually preventing me from having such an experience. By using substances, I achieved only a *temporary illusion* of safety and connectedness— plus, the substances almost killed me. After I quit using substances and gained some clarity about my true desires, I began to learn how to create experiences of well-being and love with the people in my life without needing to rely on alcohol or drugs.

My first "test" of maintaining my self-chosen state of sobriety during that Christmas party was a difficult one, but I made it through. I was able to quickly catch myself as I began to desire to drink. I immediately began to turn my attention away from the desire by examining my thoughts. That was the key to overcoming the temptation to take a drink.

Now, if I were to feel a strong desire to drink, I would begin by exploring my thoughts. I'd ask myself, "*Why* do I want to drink?" That begins a train of thought that takes me away from the strong feeling of urgency to drink. Doing this will usually lead me to a deeper understanding of my desire, and that understanding helps to make it easier for me to choose a more beneficial activity than drinking.

You can learn to use this process by training yourself to think about *what* you think. You can examine *why* you think a certain thought, and you can discover *how* you came to a certain thought or conclusion.

However, as was the case in many a therapy session I had experienced in the past, I discovered that at times this self-examination process can be overdone. Yet if you use this process wisely, then self-examination can be a very helpful tool for resolving the personal struggles involved in healing addictions and dealing with temptation—particularly when you first quit a habit.

Of course, in working with temptation in your healing process, there will be times when you will need to get away from the source of temptation. A person can stand only so much pressure, so you need to take care of yourself in that way. If you don't think you are ready to resist temptation, then avoid it.

Also, in difficult times of temptation, it helps to have an *ally*. During that Christmas holiday, my mother, who is now a great friend to me, was with me all the time. During the big family party, when everyone was drinking and having a good time, she sensed that I was struggling with temptation. She asked if I was all right, and I was able to talk to her and tell her how surprised I was that the drinks still looked so good to me—even after I had nearly killed myself with them on more than one occasion.

My mother was great. Even though it was not really necessary, she chose not to drink so I would not be the only non-drinking person at the party.

It's not a good idea to be alone with temptation when you first quit using drugs and alcohol since you might not have yet found the strength to go against your old habits. Although it's not always possible or even desired by you, it can help to have someone that you can share your frustrations with.

You can prepare yourself for temptation ahead of time by enlisting the help of a trusted friend to be with you when you go into situations where the tempting substances will be available. You can also have a list of questions ready to ask yourself when temptation attacks so you can begin the process of self-examination that will help take your attention away from the desire to use substances. That process of self-examination will also build up your inner strength, and that will serve you well in the future as you put your addictions behind you.

You can ask for help when you need it—and that includes asking it of yourself. You can make a commitment to *question* yourself and deeply explore your desire for alcohol or drugs, doing that as lovingly as you might do when trying to help a dear friend.

All of these things will help you to keep making choices that lead you toward greater health.

⌘

Chapter 23

OBSERVATION

"Are we to paint what's on the face,
what's inside the face,
or what's behind it?"

Pablo Picasso

Growing up in Southern California, where fitness has always been in fashion, I took a number of yoga classes over the years. And even though I enjoyed the classes, I was never quite able to make yoga a regular practice of mine. It just did not fit in with my lust for liquor and cigarettes.

Because I was no longer drinking, on a recent morning when I took a yoga class, my experience was different from the many other mornings I had spent at the gym or in a yoga class in the past. This time I was relieved not to have to worry about the person next to me smelling the stench of alcohol oozing from my pores.

In the past I drank so much and so often that the smell of alcohol came right through my skin. Some people think that the odor of alcohol only comes from the breath or clothes of someone who drinks a lot, but it also comes from their skin. The skin and the lungs are large cleansing organs, so it was natural that when I was saturated with alcohol, I would smell of it as my body tried to flush it out of my system. Even though it was natural, it was still something I always tried to hide. I used to stock up on those little "Breath Assure" pills, which are intended to eliminate bad breath caused by foods such as garlic and onions. But even those pills were not strong enough to hide the powerful smell of alcohol escaping from my pores.

However, during this particular yoga class, I didn't have to worry about smelling like alcohol because I had quit drinking. Instead, I had to worry about properly executing some of the more difficult yoga moves. During one particular move—a rather agonizing hip stretch that seemed to go on forever—I was about to give up and quit when the instructor announced, "This is a very strong area of the body, with lots of layers to work through, so it takes time to stretch it out." Suddenly, with that simple explanation, I was able to appreciate the exercise and continue on with it. Just by envisioning the inner workings of my body, the movement became interesting and therefore much more bearable.

Upon reflection, I could see that all it took to make the exercise more tolerable, manageable, and even enjoyable was a simple understanding of the mechanics of my body. And just as that understanding of my body got me through a difficult exercise, I learned that understanding the emotional patterns that underlie my behavioral choices can help get me through difficult inner experiences.

It was never satisfying for me to hear, *"You are an alcoholic because you have a disease,"* or, *"It's in your genes."* For me, such generic explanations of my very personal problems were no help at all. I wanted to understand what was going on with me emotionally in the way I understood what was going on with my body in the yoga class. That way, I would not feel helpless—as I could *sense* I was not.

I had made the choice to quit using alcohol and drugs. In that choice was a commitment to find out how to significantly improve my life—not merely to deny myself the use of substances. Because of that commitment, I needed a deeper understanding of my psychological patterns. So I decided that since it was me who was struggling, then I was my best subject for study. I began to carry out that study by using the powerful tool of self-observation.

Self-observation—at least in the way that I have used it to help heal my addictions—is not the same as "observing" memories of your troubled childhood or other more recent challenging events and then using those observations to explain your present difficulties, as one might do in traditional psychotherapy. Self-observation means examining your feelings and responses *as you are having them.* Memories of the *past* can often trigger feelings and responses in the *present,* but in self-observation it is not the memory that you focus on, but rather your current experience in that moment.

For example, if you suddenly feel a strong urge for a drink or a cigarette, you can begin your self-observation process by noticing what is going on in your body at that moment. Are you shaking, sweating, or is your heart racing? You might notice that it's not your heart that is racing, but rather your thoughts. Then you can start to ask yourself questions like, "I wonder why I'm feeling anxious?" Or, "I wonder what I feel is *missing* in this moment?" Maybe it's not a drink or a ciga-rette. Maybe you are missing a better *feeling* than the one you are having right now. Maybe it's a more positive feeling that you really desire, not the substance. You could also ask yourself, "Could it be I need more joyful activities in my life?" "Am I angry or sad or just feeling bad, and because of that, I want to comfort myself with a drink or a cigarette?" Then a very important question you could ask yourself would be, "Can I comfort myself in a different way that is healthier?"

There are many different beneficial questions you could ask yourself. The point is to use the questioning process along with self-observation to free yourself of the belief that drugs and alcohol are what you truly desire.

If you allow yourself to think about your answers to the questions you pose to yourself, then the process of self-observation can be very liberating. In that process you will learn that you have the power to help yourself through difficult times of craving and temptation by experiencing that ability for yourself.

At first, you might need to share your thoughts and feelings about your desire for substances with someone you trust—especially if you are, as I am, a bit stubborn and impulsive. That person can give you another viewpoint to think about, and that can lead you to even more beneficial knowledge about why you have chosen substances.

Self-observation, as I am describing it, can help you free yourself from your struggles with addictions. The more that you can learn about what drives you to behave carelessly and make negative choices in your life, the more you will be able to free yourself from those destructive behaviors.

⌘

Chapter 24

ASSISTANCE

*"We do not so much need the help of our friends
as the confidence of their help in need."*

Epicurus

*F*or the first several months after I quit drinking, it was very important for me to know that at least one person had some idea of what I was going through as I worked to put my addictions behind me. I did not want to announce to everyone that I had quit drinking, but I knew from my past failed experiences of trying to quit using substances that it would benefit me to have a person I trusted that I could talk to about the difficult experiences I knew I would go through in my quest for a healthier life.

It was also important that the person cared for

me in such a way that if I were to fail in my quest for sustained sobriety, then even if they might feel sad *for* me, they would not be disappointed *in* me. I knew it would be a great help to me if I had the support of someone who cared about me and my well-being more than my "sobriety." That would help me to trust them when they said to me that it would be so much better if I didn't drink.

There were quite a few evenings in my early days of healing when I really, *really* wanted to drink. When I would see my neighbors hanging out on their porch enjoying a beer, my craving for alcohol grew strong because I used to love to sit out on my own porch for hours—one hand holding a drink, and the other, a cigarette. Seeing other people lazing around and drinking just the way I had done was almost more than I could take. In fact, on several other failed attempts to quit drinking in the past, that type of scene had been my downfall. It would stimulate pleasant memories of alcohol—and not having the understanding I have now, I would give in.

So in the first few months of quitting my old habits, I had no desire to sit on my porch empty-handed, and non-alcoholic fruit punch was just not going to work for me. In those days, in order to resist my desire to drink and smoke, I used my television to distract me, my shower to calm me, my bed to hide me, and—very important—my ally, who cared for me and comforted me. Sometimes I needed all of those things to get through the difficult periods of temptation. I did whatever I needed to do.

These days it's much easier for me to work through a craving since I now have a lot of practice. However, in the beginning of my healing process, I really needed the support of my ally.

I often found that the easiest way to resist my strong urge to drink was to let my ally know that I was struggling. For me, it was my husband, but it can be anyone that you trust. A friend or a loved one who will try to understand you and who will not condemn you can be a great help when you are struggling with your desire to use substances. That person can remind you of the benefit of your new, healthy choices. They can also help you turn your attention away from your intense desire for substances by helping you focus on other aspects of life—a discussion of a movie, a game, world events, anything.

My husband knew how much I enjoyed sitting out on the porch, drinking, smoking and just relaxing, so he kindly commiserated with me when I missed doing those things. He understood some of the difficult thoughts and feelings I was struggling with when I gave up drinking, and he was willing to let me talk about those feelings as he helped me get through them. He helped me trust that he would always be my safety net if I felt like I was falling towards drinking again. That is what an ally can be for you. That person can be your safety net.

Even though I found that Alcoholics Anonymous did not work for me, I am able to appreciate the safety net it provides for some people. That is an important benefit of the program. In fact, it's strongly recommended that you have a sponsor—someone to be your ally. That is someone you can reach out to and rely upon twenty-four hours a day.

So if you find AA beneficial, then by all means use it. If, like me, you don't, then be sure to find an ally in your life. Find at least one person you can cry to, complain to, or run to in a desperate moment. It doesn't matter if it's your grandmother's neighbor—you need someone.

For me, it was most helpful to spend time with my ally in person, but that is not the only way to communicate and get support. You can get support through the telephone or by chatting on the Internet. In fact, at times just the knowledge that your ally is out there, waiting to care for you and support you, is enough to help you through a difficult time.

It's amazing to me how quickly I would forget the negative aspects of old habits. What happened to me—the hallucinations, the horrible depression, the extreme erratic nerves, and the agoraphobia I experienced towards the end of my drinking days—was horrifying. Yet within weeks after I quit drinking, I seriously considered, on more than one occasion, a trip to the liquor store.

Now when I get an urge to return to my old addictive habits, it helps me to remember—and talk to my ally about—why I developed those habits to begin with. Substance abuse was a way of numbing myself. I was able to prevent a bad feeling by stirring up a temporary "better" one. However, as I now remind myself, what always followed that temporary better feeling was a feeling of loss, sadness, or total misery.

There are reasons why we have urges and impulses to use drugs or alcohol. Those reasons usually revolve around wanting to *increase* a certain positive feeling or to *decrease* a negative feeling. This is important to remember so that when you desire substances, you know it's a *feeling* that you really desire, not the substance. And if you are desiring a positive feeling, then remember you can call upon your ally to help you *create* positive feelings as you are supported and cared for by that person.

So do everything you can to find at least one person to be your ally during your recovery process. The attention, support, and love of another person is usually all we need in a moment of uncertainty or despair.

⌘

Chapter 25

OPTIONS

"Still in the dress she used to wear,
faded feathers in her hair,
she sits there so refined,
and drinks herself half-blind."

Copacabana
Barry Manilow

When I was a child and still living in Santa Barbara with my dad, I would sometimes visit my mom in Los Angeles. She would take us—my brother, my sister and me—into Westwood Village for a movie. I imagine I made a terrible movie companion because I was constantly asking what time it was during the film. I was always worried that I was wasting what little time I had with my mother staring at a movie screen. I dreaded the moments when our time together

199

would be over and I would be sent back home to my loneliness and misery.

But those terrible moments of separation always came no matter how I tried to avoid them.

Since I was only eleven years old at that time, I had no understanding of what to do with my feelings of misery and the intense emotional despair that I experienced constantly, day after day. So it was during this time of deep sorrow that I began to think about killing myself. Also, I was so sad and depressed and felt so alone that I cried all the time and kept my family awake at night. I continually begged my father to let me go live with my mother.

Later, after that disruptive behavior became too much for my family to bear, my parents finally allowed me to move from Santa Barbara to live full time with my mother in Los Angeles. Being near my mother helped me to feel better, and I was not quite as depressed, but that lasted only for a short time. As much as I tried to forget and ignore the pain of the years spent living in anguish and misery without my mother, I could not. The time I had spent tormented by despair was so frightening to me that my fear of returning to that suffering was overpowering. The only way I found to get away from that fear was by using drugs and alcohol.

As a child I had dreaded being left alone because of my unusual agonizing experiences, but later, as an adult and having alcohol as my crutch, I began to look forward to being home alone. This was a big change from my earlier days as a child in Santa Barbara, when being at home, far away from my mother, terrified me. And indeed, as a young woman, home was very often the safest place for me, given that I was prone to carelessly sleep with strangers after several drinks.

Through the steady use of alcohol I was able to temporarily suppress the feelings of suffering that I feared. When I was intoxicated, I felt that my emotions were no longer at the mercy of anyone else. I had the illusion that I was in control. And to some degree, I was. I controlled whether I could sleep or not by the amount of alcohol and pills I took. I controlled my negative emotions by limiting their intensity with the numbing effects of alcohol or drugs.

However, because the emotional side effects of the drugs and alcohol were so negative, the substances actually ended up intensifying my despair rather than making it go away. So, emotionally, I was not able to hold myself together. On several occasions I ended up being hospitalized for a psychological breakdown related to my drug and alcohol use.

Also, I was in trouble physically. The ravages of substance abuse, combined with severe malnutrition from many years of starving myself, took a tremendous toll on my body. For years, I was living on the brink of death.

During those years I had many love relationships. For a brief time, those relationships helped me to lift my spirits. Temporarily, I was able to escape my sadness and despair without using drugs or alcohol. However, when the thrill of my new love was gone, I always found myself right back where I started emotionally—miserable and depressed. I would wake up one morning and find that nothing had changed except the fact that I was living with a man instead of living alone.

Each time I ended one of those relationships, I found myself searching for the bit of happiness I had temporarily gained in the relationship. Without the thrill of a new love relationship, the easiest way for me to find some pleasure was to return to my old habit of using alcohol or drugs. The result of that was that I always ended up the same way—unhappy and depressed and, as often as possible, intoxicated.

I did not feel there was a great deal of value in

any of the things I did in my life year after year, not even the occasional healthy things. There had been times as a teenager when I thought I might eventually come out of my struggles and misery and that my life might end up being a good and happy one. But by the time I hit my early twenties and my life continued to roll on in pretty much the same old miserable way, I began to lose hope for myself.

When I reached thirty-five, I was still heavily numbing myself on a daily basis. I had come to the conclusion that I would probably die that way—by my own hand, a slow suicide-by-substance. It was not that I wanted to die that way; it was that I saw no other option.

So, at thirty-five years old, I nearly surrendered my life to my destructive behaviors. I felt no hope for the future. I often said to myself—and occasionally to someone else—"Well, I guess I'll just die this way." Or, "Oh well, this was my life…too bad." Or, "I just want to die. I'm so tired of struggling."

But the truth was that I did not want to die. I wanted to *feel* better.

When a person is constantly inebriated, there are two things that are happening simultaneously: One, they are numbing negative feelings that need to be experienced in order to be healed; and two, they are experiencing extremely distorted emotions caused by the chemical effects of the drug or alcohol.

What I finally did for myself was to eliminate those distorted emotions by taking away the alcohol and drugs. Of course, that was not easy, but when I got clear of those confusing influences, to my great surprise, it turned out that the negative feelings I had been afraid of having were not as overwhelming as I had feared. I discovered that my feelings of fear had been greatly exaggerated by my heavy use of substances.

However, I was not able to quit drinking just because I suddenly discovered my emotions were not as frightening or as difficult to live with as I had believed. And it did not come about because I miraculously felt a sense of overwhelming goodness and a great new passion for life. The truth is that I decided to quit because I was terrified. I was more afraid of the "waking nightmares" brought about by my alcohol abuse than I was of my horrible depression and my troubling fears from my childhood.

Even though I had learned to live with all of the other miserable aspects of substance abuse— feeling constantly sick and hung-over, the embarrassing social behaviors, the promiscuous sexual behavior, and the financial burdens of my addictions—I found right away that I could not live with the nightmarish hallucinations that too much alcohol brought on. The horrifying hallucinations were what finally got my undivided attention. The experience of that terror is what brought me to my knees and that is what started me on my journey back to health.

But, if you are struggling with despair and addiction, you do not need to experience the kind of terror that I did in order to be motivated to change. It is much better for you to just read about my horrifying experiences with the uncontrollable waking nightmares than having to actually go through them yourself.

You have the option not to end up constantly drunk, near death, passed out in some strange place, lost, and without hope. You can learn from me—and from others who have fallen deep into terrible experiences related to their addictions and then healed themselves—that even if you feel you are living in an emotional hell, there *is* a way out. It's not magic, and you can't buy it. But the way out is always available to you. It's a matter of feeling your inner strength and creating the determination that it takes to make positive, healthy changes in your life.

Although I believed that I was doomed to end up sick, drunk and miserable, I was not. It is *never too late* to revive your spirit and to care for your body. No matter how deep you think you have sunk into the misery of addiction, all is never lost. You always have the option to discover your strength and change the choices that you make. You can lift yourself into a new, healthier life.

⌘

Chapter 26

PURPOSE

"What makes life dreary is the want of a motive."

George Eliot

Toward the end of my drinking days, shortly before the horrifying hallucination experience I described in Chapter One, I was completely depleted and exhausted. I had so little energy that it seemed easier to keep drinking than to quit—especially knowing that each time I had quit drinking in the past, my life got more miserable. My nights would be filled with more anxiety; and my days, with more worry and gloom. So in this most recent depleted state, before my final breakdown, I could not bear the thought of any more misery.

But even in my depleted, miserable state, I sensed I needed more of a purpose for my life than

I had known in the past. At that time, I felt my only purpose in life was to sustain a somewhat tolerable level of emotional comfort by numbing my negative feelings with substances. And, as it turned out, it was my discovery of my own worth and purpose that led me to quit using substances.

Initially, of course, my first new purpose was to eliminate the alcohol-induced hallucinations. Then, following that, my next new purpose was to *finally* discover why I felt so miserable in my life that I believed I needed to use substances to calm and comfort myself. I wanted to learn to be happy without using substances.

Feeling that we have a purpose in life, a positive reason to be healthier and to make changes, makes a huge difference when it comes to quitting an addictive habit. Though my initial purpose had to do with escaping a great fear, I later found many other motivating reasons not to return to my old, destructive behaviors. So from the very first day I quit using substances, even though I was still feeling terrible emotionally and physically, I began the process of opening myself up to finding more purpose in my life.

Beginning to look for purpose in my life did not mean that I suddenly discovered "the meaning of life" or that I had evolved to some higher spiritual realm. It meant I discovered there was something I wanted to do *even more* than get intoxicated: I wanted to heal my depression and end my use of substances once and for all.

If you struggle with substance dependency, it's not necessary to immediately have a strong reason for quitting. You can stop using drugs or alcohol even while you are searching for a reason to do so. I have found (and have observed with others) that the longer you allow yourself to remain free from drugs and alcohol, the more reasons you will find for doing so.

It's difficult to feel a meaningful sense of purpose when you have had many years of constant inebriation. Being in a substance-induced depression can limit your ability to feel desires for anything but that substance. But your ability to feel joy and purpose always lives within you. It does not vanish. The task of each one of us is to wake up that ability.

For many years I struggled to feel joy, and I longed to have the happiness I saw other people experiencing in their healthy activities. I wanted to enjoy those types of activities, but joy was difficult for me to feel because I had forgotten how to do so without substances. What I did not understand was that not only had I numbed my negative feelings with substances, but I had unintentionally numbed my capacity to feel the simple pleasures of day-to-day life. It's those simple pleasures that could have led me to experience more purpose in my life.

Not too long ago I was at a club, sitting at the bar with friends, listening to a blues band. The drinks were flowing. We were on the fourth or fifth round, and everyone was having a good time. I was drinking soda water with lime. I was not tempted to actually cross the line and drink alcohol, but I did begin to ask myself, "Now, what were those reasons why I don't drink?" At that moment I could not think of the reasons. But I noticed that I was enjoying the people I was with as we listened to the band. This was a moment when I realized my capacity to experience the "simple pleasures" in life was reawakening. In that overly tempting situation, I was able to resist drinking—not because I could recall all my good reasons, but because, knowing there was a larger purpose, I was able to relax and enjoy the simple pleasures—great friends and good music.

If you find yourself in a place in your life that feels as insignificant and purposeless as mine did, I encourage you to continue to seek out healthy things that interest you, satisfy you, and bring you joy. Going from a life without joy to a life filled with purpose is a process. It takes time and patience to make that transition. So if you don't immediately find joy and satisfaction when you quit drinking and you feel discouraged about that, do not give up hope. Continue to try to find your passions and to treat yourself well, knowing that, with patience and time, you can reawaken your ability to feel the joys of the simple things in life— and that can even be your purpose.

⌘

Chapter 27

REGRET

*"If I had only known,
I would have been a locksmith"*

Albert Einstein

Sometimes I wonder what my life would be like if I had managed to change all my unhealthy habits and behaviors at thirteen years old, when I was locked up for the first time in a drug and alcohol rehabilitation center. Would I have graduated from some Ivy League college *summa cum laude*—the best, with the greatest honors? Would I be dead from a fantastic injury while participating in the Olympic Games? Would I be married with two kids and have that famous white picket fence? Sometimes I wonder....

I can now say, yes, it would have been wiser to stop abusing substances at thirteen—or nineteen, or twenty-five, or even thirty. But perhaps I am a stronger and wiser person for having survived my tumultuous life spent in addictions and depression. All that I have become—the emotional strength and wisdom I have gained—would I have accomplished that any other way? I don't know. What I do know is that I'm here now. I stopped using drugs and alcohol when I did, and that is good.

When I was younger I always promised myself I would end all of my bad habits before they caused me any permanent damage. But for the greater part of my life, I was unable to do that, and my body has suffered for it. Through all of my good intentions, my prayers, my wishful thinking, and my endless therapies, I was not able to escape the pull of my addictions.

I may never know to what extent I have damaged my body. However, I can guess that it will always need a bit more attention and care than the average person who has not abused themselves the way I did in my past.

At times I have felt extreme regret about wasting my life with addictions. I have felt deep disappointment for so many of the poor choices and the mistakes I have made. In fact, I used to get caught up for hours, making mental lists of my many regrets, and the regrets seemed to be endless. I would remember something bad with one person and one incident, and then another, and another, to the point of feeling physically ill.

Not only would I feel sorry for the many people I had affected in negative ways throughout my life, but I would also feel sad for myself. I felt I had ruined my chances to have a successful life and to do something worthwhile. I knew it was too late to become a world-class athlete—or anything else that required training or schooling from a young age.

But I did more than just mourn over the many missed opportunities in my life—I constantly dwelled on them. I felt, "I blew it. I am too old and too late. I have really ruined my life." That way of thinking became another excuse for me to continue on with my life of addictions. I thought, "Why bother to quit now? My life is already ruined."

However, when I did finally eliminate substance abuse from my life, I realized there are *many* things I am still capable of accomplishing in my life. There are many things I am interested in doing. That realization did not happen for me immediately when I quit using substances, but it has happened.

I believe it can be helpful to occasionally

mourn our past in order to vent feelings of regret. But too much dwelling on the past can distract us from fully living in the present. When I'd catch myself obsessing about the past, I would remind myself the past is over and I cannot change it. But I also understood that my *feelings* about the past were not over, and it is those feelings that I needed to experience and release in order to heal.

The regret that I felt in the present about events in my past all boiled down to the same feeling—a general feeling of overall *badness* about myself. Because I can't change the past but I can work with my feelings in the present, that is what I did. In fact, it was that feeling of badness that was at the root of my substance abuse.

Eventually I came to understand that what matters, when healing feelings of regret about the past, is not so much what I *did* in the past, but what I *do* with the present feelings that are stirred up when I remember my past. I realized that if every time I felt regret, I created a feeling of being so unworthy that I believed that my life was not worth rescuing, then of course, I would never recover. But if I decided to focus on and heal my feelings of badness about myself, then I could learn to release those feelings so that I could feel encouraged and inspired to continue on in my life with healthier choices.

I have always been keenly aware of my feelings. However, I often confused my feelings with my identity—if I *felt* bad, then I thought I *was* bad. Since most of my feelings were extremely negative for so many years, I was left believing that I was bad—very bad. As I have healed and evolved out of my addictions and depression, I have come to understand that my feelings are temporary experiences and that they do not define who or what I am. I am not a feeling; I experience feelings. A person can have a bad feeling about themselves, but that does not make them a bad person.

In my healing process I have found that after I allow myself to experience that "general feeling of overall badness," I can release it and see myself as separate from it. I now understand that feelings do not damage me, and they do not characterize or define me. I only *believed* that they do.

Of course, for people who are healing addictions, feeling regret about the past is entirely understandable, given the many obnoxious, embarrassing, and even dangerous things a person is prone to do when they are intoxicated. It's normal to wish we had not done certain things in the past. However, it's important to understand that behind that feeling of regret is a fear that we are bad and that, because we are bad, we will be dismissed, rejected, condemned, and forgotten—forever.

No one wants to be condemned and abandoned. But once again, making foolish choices, which can lead us to bad *feelings* about ourselves, does not make us bad people. Thoughtless behaviors while intoxicated can make us look foolish and ignorant, but those behaviors do not make us bad people.

The other day, while I was riding my bike, I watched a bird soaring through the clouds above me. I thought to myself, "All I can tell about that bird is that it's a gorgeous bright blue color and it's flying. But for all I know, it may be a very old bird with a long, hard life of hitting windshields and fence posts. I cannot know its life. But what I can know, and what is important for me to know— and even more so for the bird—is that right now it's flying through those great big billowy clouds."

It became clear to me then that where I am *now* in my life should be my most important focus. I may need to recover and heal from some of my past experiences, but like that bird, who is still a bird and not his past injuries, I am me, healing in the present—not my bad feelings about the past.

Although it was not a simple or easy thing to

do, I have released my old negative habits, and in doing so I have found that life is a very different experience when my feelings are not so distorted by substances or substance-induced depression. I can now see that there are still many, many positive—and joyful—things that I can do for myself and for others in every moment that I am alive.

As you continue to recover your strength and stamina after long periods of depression and intoxication, it is helpful to remind yourself you are not dead; you are *living*. Working with the feelings you are presently having instead of worrying about and regretting specific events of the past can help you have a more joyful life.

⌘

Chapter 28

PRACTICE

"He who controls others may be powerful,
but he who has mastered himself is mightier still."

Lao-Tzu

About six months into my new non-drinking lifestyle, I was buying groceries at a large health food store when the checker began to get on my nerves. He was moving so slowly that, even though it was not my turn to ring out yet, I began to get really annoyed. His dawdling movements were not in sync with my fast-paced energy. Although I am usually very patient with everyone at that particular store—I never know which herbal remedy or cleansing fast they might be on that day—this guy was seriously irritating me.

When my turn came to check out, I moved

forward and watched as the checker leisurely picked up each of my items. Even though the behavior of this guy was really bothering me, as I observed him, I did my best not to show my irritation.

The checker carefully placed each of my products, one by one, in his right hand before he slowly rotated it around with his left hand to *maybe* find the price barcode. Then, *if* he was able to locate the price sticker, he would dutifully scan the item, and then with the precision of an engraver and the pace of a snail, he would place the fruit or other grocery item in a brown paper bag that he also took the time to open up for me with perfection.

To top that all off, I had to listen to the whiney soundtrack of his voice making muffled comments I could not understand. What was especially bothersome was that he seemed to be so pleased with his performance—which, to me at the time, was not pleasing at all.

As I lifted my bag into my shopping cart, he asked if I wanted to keep my drink out. I thought to myself, "No, you dope, I don't want to keep my drink out. Put it the bag with my other stuff so I can get out of here." However, what I said out loud was, "No, thanks. You can just put it in the bag."

Suddenly, as I suppressed my desire to be rude, it occurred to me that I was in total control of my feelings of irritation in that moment. I realized that in spite of my impatience, if I had thought this guy was interesting or someone I wanted to flirt with, then my thoughts and feelings would have been completely different. If I had wanted to communicate with that checker in a way that would have attracted him to me, then when he asked me if I wanted to keep my drink out, I would have said "yes" in a friendly way and reached out to take the drink, hoping my hand might brush with his. I realized that my negative experience with this guy would have been entirely different if I had seen him as a potential friend.

If I had not noticed that it was *me* who was stimulating my irritation and not the checker, I could have embarrassed myself by being insensitive. I might have rolled my eyes to the other people waiting in line, enlisting their support for my own agitation. I could even have complained to the manager and endangered the guy's job. However, I caught myself. I realized that if I had acted on my bad feelings, I would only have managed to exaggerate my frustration and that of those around me. I might even have hurt the guy's feelings, maybe even his employment. That was not my intention when I went out shopping that day—just as self-destruction was not my intention when I first began using substances to alleviate my bad feelings.

I have learned throughout my healing process that when I have a bad feeling—a feeling of aggravation or otherwise—I do not in reality require a quart of vodka and twenty cigarettes to get through that negative feeling. I now know that bad feelings are *temporary*, and that if I have the patience to take a moment to notice those feelings *before* I rush to eliminate or express them, then I can remember they are only feelings and that they require nothing more than my willingness to be with them until they pass.

That day in the health food store, my aggravation was not the fault of the checker. It had to do with the negative thoughts and feelings that were stirred up in me, *by me*. Yet I was on the verge of being obnoxious and rude to that checker, and potentially either making him feel bad or causing trouble with his employer, because I thought *he* was the cause of my troubles. He was only a young man, doing his job in his style—though a very odd style, and done at a very slow pace. Nonetheless, he was just doing his job.

In the same way that I was able to calmly and objectively notice my negative feelings about that situation, I can notice my negative feelings when I begin to think that I might like to have a drink or a drug. As a result of this new awareness of my ability to monitor my feelings, I am able to refrain from behaviors that I might later regret. I am now able to recognize that my old overwhelming desires for a drink or drug—the desires that led me to feel I might die if I did not satisfy them—were only *temporary feelings*. It's now clear that I do not die when I don't use substances.

I now know that bad feelings cannot harm me. It's very helpful for everyone to know this, especially those of us who are prone to rush to eliminate our bad feelings by using substances. We need to *practice pausing* before we act on the impulses of our feelings. That can help us gain control over our unhealthy habits.

Whenever you are in a situation that causes you to stir up negative feelings—whether shopping in the market or anywhere else you may be—practice stepping back from those bad feelings so you can realize that you are fully in charge of those feelings and what you do with them. Remind yourself that, as bad as they may feel in the moment, they are only feelings. Yes, they *feel* terrible,

but the feelings themselves will not harm you—
and they will pass.

⌘

Chapter 29

STRENGTH

"When I dare to be powerful,
to use my strength in the service of my vision,
then it becomes less and less important
whether I am afraid."

Audre Lorde

*I*nitially, during my last terrible detox episode, what motivated me to quit drinking was *fear*. I mentioned in earlier chapters that I had quit using alcohol and drugs several times before, though never for any significant period of time. The reason I believe that my previous attempts failed is because what had motivated me to quit in the past was my desire to please the people who loved me and to better fit into society, not because I thought doing so would make me feel better. I had a strong desire to be happier, but I did not have a strong desire to let go of my addictions.

During my previous and short-lived attempts at sobriety, I experienced intense aggravation, dramatic mood swings, and depression. I experienced sleepless and sweat-filled nights. My desires, especially for alcohol and cigarettes, always kept me on edge. And while all those experiences were extremely unpleasant and difficult to bear, they were not terribly frightening. It was only during my last withdrawal experience, when I had the "waking nightmares," or hallucinations, I was so terrified that my overwhelming fear essentially forced me to quit drinking.

So initially, on that last occasion, it was fear that motivated me to give up my addictions. But as I recovered my physical strength and my fear subsided, I found I needed something more than that fear to help me refrain from using alcohol and drugs. Because that fear was temporary, it was not something I could depend on to help me resist my desire to numb my emotions with substances forever. I needed to find something else, something that I could *always* depend on to support me if I ever began to feel distraught and a desire to use alcohol or drugs again.

What I found, and what I have learned to depend on to get me through difficult times of temptation and misery, is my own *inner strength and courage*. Of course, not only did I not feel strong and brave when I first quit, but I felt I might have lost what little strength and courage I had to begin with. But as I healed, I discovered I had not completely lost my strength and courage during my many years of intoxication—they were just buried beneath the despair, fears, and the cumulative effects of my use of alcohol and drugs.

I believe the same is true for everyone who is abusing substances—each one of us actually has all the inner strength we need to carry ourselves through difficult times. It's only a matter of seeking it, finding it, and using it.

Recognizing and using my inner strength is the essential element that helps me continue to abstain from using alcohol or abusing drugs. I have learned to recognize that my own strength is always there for me to draw upon whenever I need it. The important thing is to remind myself of that strength and to use it.

However, I don't try to bully myself into remembering my strength. That is not the sort of "forced" strength I require to avoid indulging in destructive behaviors. What I need is a solid foundation of unshakable certainty that I have all the strength and wisdom I need to make healthy choices in my life.

So, to help formulate that sense of certainty, I say to myself:

> "I know I have passed through and overcome many difficult and terrible experiences. I know I have struggled deeply and painfully. But I also know I have gained tremendous emotional 'muscle' from those experiences. This is true whether I can feel it or not."

After that, what I do, to the best of my ability, is to *feel* that emotional 'muscle,' that inner strength I have gained.

No matter what drives you to quit an addiction, whether it is fear, social pressure, or family intervention, it's important to remember that it is your inner strength that enables you to quit using substances. I believe the important thing is not *what* originally brings you to quit—it is the strength and courage that *you* bring to sustain your new healthy habits.

This is not as difficult as you might think. It's a matter of becoming aware of a kind of inner power that already exists within you. You need to know that it is within your power to overcome addictive habits. The strength that is required to do that *already lives within you.* I did not always believe that, but I can now see clearly that it was always true.

Learn to feel your inner strength and build upon it by noticing when you have made it through a difficult situation. Not only is it a great comfort to know that your inner strength is there for you anytime you want to call upon it, but you will also find that you will use it constantly in many areas throughout your life.

In my past, I was deeply attached to my self-destructive habits, and like a raggedy old security blanket, I found it nearly impossible to completely let go of those habits. In the beginning, I needed every bit of strength I could find in order to resist the strong urges and temptations that confronted me daily. And at times, what was even more difficult than the physical presence of a drink or drugs were my *thoughts* about a drink or drugs. I not only had the habit of drinking, but I also had the habit of thinking about drinking. I had to have a great deal of trust that I had the strength to change my mental habits. I had to trust that in time it would get easier for me to let go of the habit of constantly thinking about alcohol and drugs.

I found that my inner strength has been absolutely essential in my recovery. And it is one of the biggest rewards of my hard work. My awareness of my inner strength sustains me in many ways and in many areas of my life.

I believe this can be true for everyone. If you take the time to encourage yourself to feel the inner strength that already lives within you, then you will be able to experience the great benefits of that strength. I am convinced that if you suffer from addictions as deeply as I have—or even more than I have—you can also learn to experience the gift of your inner strength and bring it forward to be your constant source of support in your new life of better health and well-being.

⌘

Chapter 30

TRANSITION

"Once, during Prohibition,
I was forced to live for days
on nothing but food and water."

W.C. Fields

It is a miserable feeling to be suddenly without a habit that you have been so deeply attached to. The abrupt withdrawal of a long-held habit can leave a person feeling disoriented, agitated, and afraid.

When this last happened to me, I had a very difficult time adjusting to it. I had trouble making commitments to social events or outings. Something that might seem so simple for some people, such as having dinner with friends, was an ordeal for me. It was something I needed to think a lot about before I made my decision to go or not. I did not want to experience the frustration of sitting through a meal without wine. I knew I would be bothered as my thoughts wandered over to my plain glass of water, wishing it were wine.

In the early months of withdrawal from my addictive habits, I was so full of worry about my life—my physical health, my living circumstances, my future without alcohol or cigarettes—that the last thing I felt I needed was more aggravation. So in order not to add any more pressure to the already stressful process of ending addictions, I tended to just avoid situations that made me feel too anxious or upset. In the earlier stages of my withdrawal, I kept myself as comfortable as possible until I felt strong enough and calm enough to be in an environment that might test my new behavior of not drinking or using drugs.

In the past, my choice would have been much different. I seldom put myself in a position where I *could not* have a cigarette or a drink. Even if I had to hide it, I made sure that something—even a type of alcohol I would not normally choose to consume—was available to me. I was like all those people you see in the movies that hide their liquor bottles. I even had my own flask. I also carried with me my trusty bottle of anti-anxiety medication for when my nerves became too much to handle. Without my "fixes" I did not socialize very well. I was always thinking about where I could get a drink and a smoke.

Ending drug or alcohol addictions can be one of the most difficult things a person will ever do. The psychological pull to return to using substances can be so overwhelming that it is, at times, irresistible for some. That is why it can take a person several tries before they are successful. It's hard to do, but it is possible to do it. However, it takes a great deal of determination and strength and a willingness to feel bad, or at least uncomfortable, for a certain period of time.

If you were enjoying a nice warm shower and someone suddenly turned off the water, it would be difficult to stand there, shivering cold, your body covered in sticky, drying soap, and you, without a clue as to what happened or when and how you could get the water back on. For an addict, withdrawal can be much, much worse than that physically uncomfortable and psychologically confusing situation in the shower. Withdrawal from addiction can *feel* intolerable.

That is why I believe that gently easing our way out of addictions is the best way to heal from them. What that means—easing your way out—is that the transition from being constantly inebriated to being completely sober is *made easier* by giving yourself healthy, comforting, and loving gifts during the process of letting go. Easing out of an addiction does not mean allowing yourself two martinis instead of twelve. It means doing everything possible to make the transition easier.

If the process of letting go of addictions can be made an easier one, then the attractiveness of quitting will be much greater. You will be more likely to attempt it and more likely to succeed. This certainly was true for me.

When I quit drinking I needed as much comfort as possible—it was the only way I was able to make it through some of my more disturbing moments of anguish as I struggled with extremely strong desires to use substances. I discovered that what I really needed in those moments of anxiety and fear was not actually the drink or the drug. What I really needed was to know that I was going to be okay. I needed to feel that I was safe, and that I would be all right, and even better, if I did not drink or use drugs. Sometimes I would receive that reassurance from a physician, and sometimes from a loved one. However, the most reliable source of reassurance turned out to be *me*. If nothing else, I was always around.

The way I worked to comfort myself and to convince myself that I was going to be okay was, first, to create reassuring thoughts. I would also give myself as many tangible gifts as I could: comfy pajamas, soothing food, movies in bed, massage whenever possible, new soaps, and anything else I could think of to bring alternative pleasurable sensations. The more I was able to calm myself and release my fears of impending danger with those gifts, the more encouragement, joy, laughter, and fun I was able to allow myself to feel.

Learning to comfort myself took some practice, but it was not as difficult as I thought it would be. It was only a matter of remembering the importance of being extra kind, generous, and loving toward myself during that difficult period of adjustment. I learned that actively and consistently giving myself small gifts of kindness *actually worked* to ease the difficulties of giving up an addiction.

In the past, I felt it was impossible to sit through an entire meal and conversation without a drink, or at least a break for a cigarette. But it was not long before I proved to myself that I *could* sit through dinners and conversations without terrible anxiety and without feeling I needed to flee. I did that by offering myself an alternative—another way I might be able to relieve my anxiety. I thought of past experiences, when I was able to feel calm and content without being intoxicated or medicated. That helped to remind me that I am capable of feeling good without ingesting substances.

If you find yourself in a situation that makes you feel extreme nervousness and a strong desire to run off and drink or take drugs, it may help you to remember that there are other ways to calm your emotions besides using drugs and alcohol. You can try remembering a moment when you were not intoxicated, yet you felt safe and secure. Even if that occurred years ago, try to remember the feeling. You may have been a child, curled up safe under a blanket with a flashlight. You might have been an adult, in the arms of a loved one. It doesn't matter what memory you use. What matters is that you learn that you are capable of creating feelings of calm and goodness by means other than substances.

If you have no comforting memories, then start creating some. Give yourself small gifts of kindness throughout each day and soak up the good feelings when you experience them. Begin to build up your "bank account" of good feelings and memories so that in times of anxiety you can reach into that bank account and know that there are more ways than one to make yourself feel good.

Learning to let in feelings of goodness from your own gifts of kindness can take some time and practice, so be patient with yourself. It's important when quitting addictions that you do not feel forced or rushed to feel better. For myself, I needed to feel that I had the space and the time to go through whatever I needed to go through in order to fully recover and heal. However, I will say that the sooner you begin to practice calming yourself with generous acts of kindness and love, the easier the rest of the transition period will be.

⌘

Chapter 31

ꟿNDEPENDENCE

"My head explodes, my eyes ring,
I can't remember just where I've been.
The last thing that I recall,
I got lost in a deep black hole.
Don't want to find out
Just want to cut out."

Blackout
Scorpions

Sometimes, in order to find a reason to make a change in our lives, we condemn and blame those around us. In a love relationship it can look like this: The man or the woman is feeling restless or bored in their life, so they decide to break up, move out, and move on. In order to feel justified in that decision, the person becomes very critical of the other's behavior, habits, and so on. This gives them that added boost and "courage" to make the final break. They have degraded that person so much in their mind, and probably to a friend or two as well, that they can feel leaving is justified and morally correct.

This can work for a while—until their new lover begins to bore them also. Then they begin to criticize and exaggerate the negative things in the new person so that they can again feel justified in their decision to leave. They may even try to return to the first lover, who in comparison is looking pretty good again.

That same pattern can be applied to using alcohol or drugs or cigarettes—and it has the same result as it does with lovers: The pattern repeats itself until it is recognized and changed.

Every time in the past when I quit smoking cigarettes, I started smoking again in spite of the many times I reminded myself of the terrible and unhealthy consequences of smoking. I thought about my friend's father who had emphysema and could hardly breathe. I told myself how the ciga-rette companies were using me to make money. I told myself how disgusting I was and that nobody smokes in California anymore so it was even more terrible that I smoked. And just like the way one would condemn a lover to justify leaving, I held nothing back when condemning those nasty, evil cigarettes. But it never worked.

What did work, and what it eventually came down to, was me *choosing what I wanted*—in this case, to be a healthy nonsmoker. Simply condemning cigarettes was never enough to stop me from smoking them.

When I list the detrimental effects of alcohol, the list is long. I have seen pictures of the results of cirrhosis of the liver, and it's a horrible sight. There are many factors that *should* cause a person not to want to drink. Alcohol can lead to strokes, dementia, brain damage, delirium tremens, cancers, automobile accidents, kidney damage, dangerous sex—and the list goes on. However, for someone like me, someone who was so deeply entrenched in the habits of drinking, listing those frightening possibilities was helpful only *after* I had already quit for a while.

Trying to make the alcohol itself the problem never worked to make me quit drinking it. However bad it was, I liked to drink alcohol—lots and lots of alcohol. It was the same with smoking. In fact, most people I have talked to that smoked for a long period of time and finally managed to quit have said the same thing, *"I liked smoking."* To change something that I once enjoyed into something completely nasty was attempting to force myself to believe what I knew was not true, and that did not work for me.

Making alcohol something to fear in order to keep from drinking it was not my way to quit drinking either. I do not like the idea of spending the rest of my life feeling weak in relation to a substance—and I will not. The problem is what I choose to do with substances, not the substances themselves. Substances will always be around, so it does not seem to me that running from them is a solution. To make substances my problem, my reason for being addicted to them, meant to me that I was building on fears rather than what I really needed to do, which was to build on my own strength and independence.

Of course, there are times when our fear of alcohol's seduction is so great that we *should* avoid alcohol or drug-related situations. I remember being in a club to hear some music soon after I quit drinking and smoking. The smell of tobacco mingled with beer was so great that I just had to get out of there—period.

However, as my strength increased, I learned to address my fears related to drinking and smoking so I do not need to live my life in fear of substances. I recently went to a concert given by a band that I've loved since I was a teenager. During the show the smell of marijuana and beer was constant and strong. But I was so happy to be at the concert, and so strong in my commitment to not return to the misery I had experienced for most of my life, that the scents didn't bother me at all.

At the concert, someone gave us backstage passes. Had I been living my life in fear of substances, I would not have been able to go backstage, where I knew there would be many temptations. Also, had I still been using substances, I would have missed out on the fun because, knowing me, I would not have remembered a thing from that night.

So when you first quit drinking, it may be necessary and wise to avoid certain situations out of fear. But it's very much to your advantage to learn to release the fears you have associated with substances while you work to increase your feelings of strength and independence. You will have to use your own good judgment on this. If you are uncomfortable being in a bar, don't go to a bar. Don't allow yourself to be tempted beyond your capacity. That means that if you are feeling uncertain or nervous about being around certain tempting situations or substances, then avoid them. That will not always be possible to do, but at times, when you are in danger of giving in to temptation, pondering the whys is not so important, and avoidance is best. Whenever possible, give yourself a break. Don't even deal with temptation—go someplace else.

When I first started drinking and using drugs, it was not because I wanted all the bad things that come with doing that. I wanted all of the good feelings and experiences that I thought were possible, and that I sometimes experienced. I had no intention of having the horrifying DT's like those I experienced at the end of my using days.

What I set out to do, after that last horrible withdrawal, was to see if I could experience great pleasure without alcohol and drugs or overindulgence in sex or food. I was trying to discover if it was possible for me to achieve a sense of contentment and joy in just being *myself.* That meant that instead of condemning substances and holding them responsible for my difficult circumstances, I sought out things I knew had made me happy in the past without being intoxicated—things such as dancing, drawing, singing, and writing. I worked to bring more of those experiences into my life.

I believe that in order to fully regain our freedom and independence from drugs and alcohol, we need to understand that a substance has the power to alter our physical bodies—and that is all. The deciding factor in whether or not we ingest that chemical lies in our own hands.

It may be useful at times to remind yourself of the detrimental effects of using drugs and alcohol. But if you notice that condemning the substance itself is not very effective in squelching your desire for it, don't feel as if you are weak or bad because that knowledge doesn't work for you. Remember the repeated pattern of the unhappy lover—criticizing another, or a substance, may not be your solution. Deciding what you want in your life can be. It's much more effective to notice what brings you joy, to discover healthier pleasures, and to invite more of those experiences into your life. I believe *that* is the best way to help yourself out of addiction and misery. It worked for me, and I believe it can work for you.

⌘

Chapter 32

REMINDERS

*"We have to use memories,
otherwise we would not find our way home.
When we use memories, we are creators.
But when our memories use us,
we become victims."*

Deepak Chopra

A few years ago I had an unusual job of putting special-effect contact lenses into the eyes of actors on the sets of television shows and movies. I worked on various vampires, monsters, and other bizarre creatures or people.

For the record, I never drank while I was on the job. I always waited until the second I got home—even if it was 2:00 in the morning. Occasionally when I was working, I did take an anti-anxiety pill, but that did not interfere with my work. If anything, it improved my skill at sticking my fingers in people's eyes.

In my brief life as a fashion model, I had experienced many photo shoots with the still camera, but working on a movie or television shoot, as I did with the lenses, was a larger production. There were more people, and much more equipment was involved, so I was able to learn a great deal more about film production than when I was modeling.

My job of working with the lenses was unique in that it enabled me to spend time with just about everyone on the shoot—the producers, the directors, the actors, the cinematographers, the soundmen, the makeup artists, the hairstylists, the caterers, the lighting technicians, and my personal favorite, the stuntmen. I wasn't a big talker, so I was able to listen and observe quite a lot, and I learned a great deal about what goes into making movies. At times I was even able to enjoy that job. The creativity, humor, and skills that were involved could often be quite entertaining. At other times, of course, the hours dragged on as they can do with any job.

Although that job was a few years ago, there are many things I learned there that will always be in my memory. I am reminded of those things every time I turn on the television or watch a film. I find it nearly impossible to watch a movie or television show without thinking about what went into making those images—the lighting, the positioning of the props, and the cues or directions I imagine the actors might have been given. Even if I tried, it doesn't seem possible that I could forget what I now know about making movies.

The same is true for my personal life—my personal life spent in addiction. I cannot forget my memories of that life and all that I know about it. There are too many reminders, and any one of them can trigger a memory. I can see a string of spaghetti and remember twenty drunken stories of me having consumed too much wine or beer during a dinner. My dog can remind me of my drinking days, my hair can remind me, vodka bottles definitely remind me—but even a warm breeze can remind me. There is no way for me to escape reminders of my troubled past. However, there is a way for me to live gracefully with the reminders of my past.

I have built an imaginary library in my mind where I store my memories, my past experiences. I have learned how not to think too much about any one experience unless I deliberately choose to. All of my memories are alive in me, but I have put them away, archived in my imaginary library. In that way I am able to maintain my present thoughts so that they are not constantly disrupted by the potentially overwhelming and upsetting presence of some very disturbing memories from my past.

This may sound a bit simple, but it actually works well for me. I came to the conclusion a long time ago that because it was impossible to escape the memories of my past experiences, I needed to find a way that I could live with them. I have had many occasions to pull out old stories for entertainment purposes or to make a point in a conversation. However, if I didn't have a sense of authority over my often disturbing stories, then thinking about them too much would be a potentially dangerous habit.

For example, if I were to notice a big, beautiful blue bottle of SKYY Vodka sitting on someone's counter and I started to dwell on my memories of the many pleasant hours I spent sitting on my balcony overlooking the Pacific Ocean and being completely free to drink as much of that bottle as I desired, it's likely I would end up, unnecessarily, in a very dark place. I might end up being overly tempted by those pleasant memories and therefore begin drinking again and making myself very sick.

Potentially, those pleasant memories might lead me to other, more disturbing memories I have that are associated with drinking vodka, such as when I ended up in the psychiatric ward of Cedars-Sinai Medical Center, held on a suicide watch for overdosing on alcohol and physician-prescribed medications.

That pretty blue glass bottle can lead me to many different places—if I allow my thoughts to go there. The trick is to learn constructive, creative ways to work with thoughts, feelings, and memories instead of trying to run and hide from them.

When I was barely a teenager, I was drinking at a friend's house in Venice Beach, when his mother came home unexpectedly and we had to make a mad dash out his bedroom window—his second-story bedroom window. The ring on my middle finger got caught on the windowsill, and it made a deep cut in my finger. I ended up at the UCLA hospital emergency room, having several stitches put in my finger.

Of course, I can't make the UCLA hospital disappear from the face of the earth just because it reminds me of that difficult period of my life, and I don't like to be reminded. And I am definitely not going to attempt to surgically erase the scar on my middle finger which, when I notice it, reminds me of that very unpleasant night in the emergency room. What I *can* do—and what has really worked for me in handling my many troubling memories—is practice containing those memories in my emotional library.

That library is stacked full of many, many memories. Whenever I want to use any of them—such as in the writing of this book—I can pull down the memories that I want from storage, do what I want with them, and then, when I am done, put them back in my library.

Where you choose to store your memories does not need to be in an imaginary library. You can use any image—a shoebox, a cave, a house, a dog house, or whatever you like.

These are mental tricks that may seem simple, but working with my thoughts in this way actually helps me feel okay about my troubling memories of the past. It helps me not to obsess on certain feelings of sadness, dread, anger, or despair so that I don't fall into depression again. And it helps me work with any memories of the pleasures that I had through my addictions by not exaggerating them so much that I want to start using substances again.

Though this mental technique of storing my

memories in my imaginary library works for me, I must on occasion still remind myself not to pull down and obsess on a memory such as, "Amy Gets Wasted and Passes Out on the Hood of a Stranger's Car" for no reason other than to make myself feel bad. That is very important. It's not a good idea to use our memories against ourselves. It's okay to use them for learning and growth—or for sheer entertainment—but never to make ourselves feel bad.

We do not need to be afraid of our memories. We only need to recognize that it's not usually a wise choice to dwell on them too much—particularly those memories related to using substances. There is another way to live with unpleasant memories that doesn't involve being afraid of them or trying to force them out of awareness. That is to acknowledge them, laugh or moan about them, and then put them back on the library shelf where they belong.

Sometimes my memories seem to emerge on their own, uninvited. This can happen while listening to a certain song or driving past an old liquor store where I used to shop. But now I know it is possible to accept and experience a bit of those memories as a part of my history without allowing myself to feel bad about myself. I am able to do this now because I know that I am in charge of those feelings and what I do with them. I can remember them for a few minutes, and then I can put them away until—if ever—I need them for some constructive purpose.

And regarding the movies and what I know about the making of them—well, maybe I *would* like to forget all of that during a really good movie. But then again, if it's a really good movie, I do forget.

⌘

Chapter 33

OTHERS

*"I've had a perfectly wonderful evening.
But this wasn't it."*

Groucho Marx

I had a dream this morning. I dreamt I was riding my bike behind my mom and her friend, who were walking along a path. They had been talking about me and were very cheerful when I approached. As we went on, I didn't notice that they had lured me into the lobby of a mental institution. The instant I realized where I was, I went on full alert, and my defenses went up.

Up until that point in the dream, I had been unusually cheery and content. But now, in the lobby of the mental institution, where I was suddenly wearing a flimsy hospital gown, that mood was lost.

Near the exit door where I was standing, I noticed a guy sitting quietly, and I secretly signaled for him to give me his shirt so I could escape. He signaled back, and carefully, so that no else one could see, he took off his shirt and gave it to me.

I saw my mom and a weaselly looking little man, who was a doctor, come out from behind a door on the other side of the room. My mom asked me to come over there for a minute. I thought to myself, "*No way!*" I knew the two of them were trying to trap me. So I replied cautiously, "Noooo…. You come over here to me."

"Come on, Amy," my mother beckoned.

"No," I said, and swiftly escaped through the sliding glass door behind me.

Then I was standing in the parking lot, and I saw my mother following after me along with that suspicious looking doctor and a huge security guard. The doctor and the security guard were both holding gigantic syringes with extremely large needles, and they were both rushing toward me.

I was thinking, "Okay. I've got a shirt now. I can try to run, or…I can beg."

I decided to beg. I pleaded with the guard and the doctor to let me talk to my mom, just for five minutes. "Please, just five minutes," I said, putting on my most rational face.

My mom spoke up and said, "No!" and grabbed the needle from the doctor.

Then she shot herself with the drugs.

I saw the security guard still standing there with his needle, ready to stick me. Looking at his size and how strong he appeared, I could see I was not going to get away.

As I stood there, feeling the terror of my ominous fate closing in on me, I struggled and woke myself up from the dream.

That dream was very upsetting because I have real memories of similar feelings I have had in the past. I remember that in my past, whenever I was confronted with my substance abuse, extremely nervous sensations would rise up and spread throughout my body. I would be overwhelmed by feelings of guilt and fears of condemnation, imprisonment, and doom. Those feelings came from real-life experiences I had where physical entrapment did occur and I did have powerful feelings of shame and fear. I had feelings of dread that came from the terror I felt about the possibility of losing what I had depended on for so many years—alcohol and drugs.

All of that was about *my* experiences, *my* fears,

and *my* feelings. On the flip side of that were the experiences, fears, and feelings of the people who loved me and cared about me. For example, I know my mother loves me deeply and always has. I did not always believe that when I was a child, but now I am certain that it was always so. I understand now that when she and the man that she was married to at the time tricked me into going into that first drug and alcohol treatment center when I was just thirteen years old, they did it because my mom was terrified of losing me. At that time I was totally caught up in my feelings of anger, gloom, and fear, but now I realize that she had some of the same kinds of feelings.

Many times, particularly in the first few months after I quit using substances, I could feel my blood rise whenever someone I cared about would mention my extreme alcohol consumption and disturbing behaviors of the past. Even though they were speaking *to* me, it felt like they were only speaking *about* me. It was as if they were talking about someone else—another entity. I can understand that being intoxicated or deeply depressed was not a true expression of myself, but it was still me they were talking about. Yes, I had made a great deal of improvement and progress, but some people assumed that now I was unshakable and could easily bear any burden. That was not true. It hurt to once again be confronted with my past behaviors that also represented my struggles. I was not ready then, and I may never be ready to talk at length about myself in that hurtful way.

On the other hand, I knew there were no ill intentions from my friends or family when they mentioned my past. I was aware that they did not intend to be insensitive; they were intending to express their joy at my great accomplishment.

It's useful to remember that our loved ones also have a journey of recovery from our years of substance abuse. Just as we need them to be patient with us, we should also be willing to be patient with them.

Since I had spent the greater part of my life in depression, therapy, and rehab and had several previous attempts at sobriety, it was understandable that those around me would not have complete confidence in my newfound ability to refrain from using alcohol or drugs. When I felt confronted by others in my recovery, to help myself be more patient with them, I reminded myself that they did not suddenly change the moment I changed.

We need to realize that, just as we had a difficult time letting go of our old habits, others might have a difficult time letting go of their attitudes and ideas about us. In fact, even though they might totally support what we are doing, some people may feel *very uncomfortable* with our changes because it requires them to make adjustments in their behavior as well. But just as it's best if we're allowed the freedom to experience our feelings and emotions throughout our ordeal without being judged, those around us also need to be given time to adjust to our new, healthier behaviors without us judging them.

About six months after I quit, I was asked by a family member to housesit for a few weeks. Just before I left to go to the house, I received an e-mail saying, "...as long as you're *really* not drinking." I was truly surprised by that message. In fact, I felt insulted. I couldn't believe I wasn't trusted.

But there was something that I had not considered—other people cannot read my mind or my heart. Because I had been so calm and sure about myself, I just assumed that everyone else would feel that way too. I had to remind myself that the people around me had not gone through what I had gone through—at least not in the same way. They did not know the depth of my dedication.

Even though it can be disappointing not to have complete understanding and support from others in this regard, it is crucial to remember to trust in ourselves and in our commitment to our newfound self-care. We can learn to let the fears, doubts, and insecurities of others fall off us like water on a raincoat. It's important to keep our new feelings of strength and confidence separate and protected from contamination by the fears and insecurities of others. Since it's possible for the worries of others to cause us to have "sobriety-threatening" insecurities, we need to make sure not to allow the doubts and negative opinions of others become our permission to fail. Instead, we can learn to ignore any suspicions, false accusations, or painful misunderstandings that others might bring to us.

Buttons will get pushed. You may feel an inner pressure or tension that stirs up a desire for a drink. That desire comes from an urge to free yourself from an emotional noose. Do not confuse the need to feel free from the pressure of others with a need for a drink or a drug. What you are feeling is a need for free expression, which is beneficial. It is not a need to drink, which would of course be detrimental.

On occasion, I would hear from various

people things like, "Really, not even one itty, bitty little sip? Come on, you can tell me." When people say things like that, it can be aggravating and confusing. It can feel as if the one asking is intentionally trying to stir up our insecurities. In situations like that, it's important to remember that what matters is not what *they* think, but what *you* think. When I experienced times like that, I reminded myself that *I* was the one who made the changes, and *I* am the one who will sustain those changes regardless of anyone else's doubts or opinions.

Ideally, if family or friends were to offer genuine, helpful support, they would express it as excitement, curiosity, patience, and kindness. But if they don't do that, and you receive suspicious, hostile, or unsupportive responses instead, re-member the times that person has tolerated your distorted behaviors over the years of your intoxica-tion, and try to do the same for them.

If you can't do that, then avoid the people who are not being sensitive to you. But try to understand that they are going through a re-adjustment process as well. There is no one who *always* says or does the perfect thing—not even you. The key to healing in all areas of your life will be kindness, compassion, and love. So, think about that, and try to go easy on the people who love you—even if they fail to support you with the perfect sensitivity and understanding that you might have hoped for.

⌘

Chapter 34

ℛEVIVAL

"The most powerful agent of growth
and transformation is something much more basic
than any technique: it is a change of heart."

John Welwood

Even though I have lived long enough to know that difficult life experiences are unavoidable, it was crushing for me when I had to put my dog down recently. I think I had hoped that when I quit drinking, my life would become miraculously easier. As it turned out, in some ways it got even more difficult.

It wasn't just letting go of my most beloved animal friend of almost thirteen years that was so difficult. It was also caring for my sister while she was undergoing treatment for breast cancer. Then there was a near divorce from my husband, our reconciliation, and finally, his diagnosis of prostate cancer.

All of these things overlapped in the same year and nearly overwhelmed me. It was a *very* stressful time. But I did not drink. In fact, I was more sober than I had ever been in my life, even though I was struggling through terrible feelings that were as challenging as the ones of my childhood.

But I was no longer a child, and my experience of emotional pain was very different. I was *capable* of coping.

As a child, I suffered through emotions that were so frightening to me that I was nearly driven to suicide. The constant pain from my feelings of sadness was so great, I thought I might need to end my life in order to stop it. I was eleven years old.

When I was finally able to move to Los Angeles to live with my mother, I had a brief period of bliss. Reuniting with her was monumental for me because the many difficulties of my childhood seemed to suddenly disappear.

But even in my temporary bliss, I was not really at peace. Every second I carried with me a dread that my terrible feelings of despair and panic might return. Earlier, I described those feelings as my "bubble feeling." Today, more than 25 years later, I can still remember making a solemn promise to myself during that slight reprieve that I would never, no matter what, allow myself to go through that horrible bubble feeling experience again. Never.

I had no idea at the time what a life-altering and life-threatening promise I had just committed myself to. For years and years I turned to substances to keep my feelings under control. In my desperate attempt to avoid my terrible feelings, I came close to dying several times. Deliberately numbing my mind and body by carelessly consuming drugs, alcohol, and food in order to avoid my feelings of despair was a dangerous way to live.

It was also a miserable way to live. Some parties were fun, some moments were exciting, but mostly the life I experienced during the many years I spent intoxicated was miserable, empty, and void of the peace of mind I had originally sought when I began turning to substances to ease my emotional pain.

I have finally learned that just because I *felt* incapable of dealing with frightening thoughts, feelings, and emotions—and so chose to numb myself with substances—does not mean I was not *capable* of dealing with them in a healthy, conscious way. I am not saying it's a fun thing to do. In fact, the times when I have dealt with difficult emotions in a healthy way were not fun at all. But to become fully alive again, to uncover the best of who you are, it's necessary to handle certain emotionally trying experiences while you are fully conscious—that is, sober.

During this most recent series of difficult events, I did not drink alcohol, attempt suicide, or do anything else that was detrimental, as I had always done in the past. I managed to hang on, eat fairly well, and accomplish whatever had to be done, especially helping the people who needed me.

I cried when I needed to—sometimes with others, more often alone. Instead of stuffing my pain away, I tried to create some positive feelings to keep myself going. Even though the stress I was under made that especially difficult, in those depressing and challenging circumstances, I was able to recognize and accept that period of my life for what it was—another extremely difficult time, but not one that would destroy me. I handled my daily life the best I could, reassuring myself that things would get better eventually. And they have.

There are certain events in life that we have no control over, such as other people's cancer and the death of a loved one. Yet, we *can* have control over how we handle ourselves through those kinds of extreme experiences. We can choose to get wasted or in other ways try to ignore the facts of the life that is unfolding around us. But, like holding a finger in a hole in a dam that is about to explode, that is not solving the problem. The pressure of our feelings and the situation will build up and eventually burst, resulting in things like poor physical health, crippling depression, destructive relationships, and financial loss. When those types of crushing experiences happen one after the other, it is often called "hitting bottom," or, "rock bottom." Some people never learn how to recover from an experience like that. But you can.

It is a matter of believing there is enough goodness within you so that you are able to ignite your will in order to keep searching for solutions. If you can learn to trust that there truly is goodness and love within you, then eventually you can create experiences of goodness and love. You will be able to see yourself more clearly, and you will see that you are a good and important person.

Throughout this book, I have stressed the importance of being kind and compassionate toward yourself as you let go of what I believe is one of the most difficult habits to end—using substances to cope with challenging feelings. It *is* difficult, but it *can* be done. I am proof of that.

How did I manage to get through the many overlapping and deeply painful experiences that I recently faced without numbing myself? Some people say that if it were not for a certain therapeutic program or a certain inspiring person in their life, they never could have survived. I say that without the inner foundation I created for myself—the *change of heart* I have experienced and that I carry with me in every moment—I never would have made it.

In order to have realistic expectations, it's important to know that the change of heart I had did not happen overnight. But what did happen overnight was my decision to be patient and wait for it.

Of course, when I first quit drinking, I didn't know exactly what I was waiting for. But I was determined to find out. I knew there had to be something better than the terrible, empty experiences I had when I was sober in the past.

I am finally able to say with confidence that there *is* something better than the empty experience of life I used to have when I wasn't drinking or using drugs. There is a foundation of love inside each of us that we can experience. When we clean off the mud of unhealthy substances and fears, we can know and feel that love.

It is that foundation that gave me the confidence I needed to pull myself through my recent difficult circumstances and feelings without numbing myself. That solid foundation can help pull each of us through any challenge we must face. When you discover that foundation, you will have your change of heart.

⌘

Living without drugs and alcohol means becoming emotionally raw and vulnerable to pain. For this reason, there is a very good chance that when you first quit drinking or using drugs, you will feel miserable. The problem now will not be how will you sneak down your next bottle of vodka, but how will you live consciously with all your emotions and sensitivities, no matter how bad they make you feel.

In my experience, recovery from years of habitual substance abuse takes longer than the typical thirty days allotted in most rehab facilities. That number is based on what insurance companies are willing to pay, not on what a person truly needs.

Because growth of any kind takes time, patience on your part is essential. A willingness to just tolerate feeling crappy sometimes is essential.

I have learned that it's possible not to feel so frightened of experiencing bad feelings, whether it's the sheer terror of panic or more mild feeling of anxiety. I have also learned that I do not need to immediately rush to avoid those feelings. Instead, I can take as much time as I want to experience what is going on inside of me, without being frightened that my bad feelings are going to harm me in some way.

As I mentioned earlier in this book, conscious unwise actions are triggered by fearful feelings. The bad feelings themselves will never harm us. It can help to view those feelings as a necessary part of the cleansing and healing process of your mind and body. It can also help to understand that a bad feeling is not in itself wrong or harmful. It's what we *think* about each feeling that makes it good or bad.

The same is true about people. You can think that a sensitive person is weak and inferior, or you can think that a sensitive person is lucky because they are able to experience life on a much deeper and more rewarding level than those who are insensitive. However, no matter what *you* think, that sensitive person remains sensitive.

And so it is with feelings. The more you think

that a certain feeling is frightening, horrible, and bad, the more frightening, horrible, and bad it will *feel.* But that does not make the feeling itself bad. Our opinion is what makes a personality trait or a feeling "good" or "bad."

Of course, we are all pretty much in agreement with some opinions, such as dental work hurts and we would like to avoid it as much as possible. However, in order to relieve the pain of a toothache, and oftentimes to save a tooth, we need to experience a certain degree of pain, even if it's just the hurt of the needle from the anesthetic shot.

It is the same with difficult emotions. To heal hurtful feelings, sometimes we just have to feel them. If you can accept that your *opinion* of what is bad is what makes negative feelings seem so bad, then you will be able to calm your feelings of fear. When you're able to calm your feelings, there won't be such a need to use substances to numb them.

I recently saw a television news show about a boy who was being treated for brain cancer. The reporter was amazed at the young boy's strength and courage, and he asked the boy if he was just putting on a show for the cameras. The boy said that he was not. He said that he really did feel strong. He told the reporter that he used to be the type of kid who was afraid of needles. He went from being frightened of needles to having the great strength and courage it takes to face serious surgeries, radiation, and chemotherapy. It was not the needles that changed—they actually got worse. It was the boy's feelings about the situation.

If you have read this book from the beginning and you still feel afraid that you cannot change, I strongly encourage you to question that *belief.*

Sometimes, it takes a certain new insight or experience to motivate us to make changes. If you have not found what you need in my book, do not give up hope or stop looking for what will work for you. We are each unique individuals, and people and events can have a different impact on each of us.

Keep searching for what works for you. Look for a mentor. Go to recovery meetings if that helps you. But always look for what helps you feel your *own* strength, and your *own* abilities. Then you can learn that you can sustain yourself in any emotionally difficult moment, and in any emotionally trying circumstance without artificial support.

Whatever you do, do not believe you are ruined. Do not believe you are beyond saving. You can change the way you feel and behave. You can bring color and joy into your life. You can feel good about what you do and who you are. And even if you cannot believe that now, in time, after you have let go of your old destructive habits, you will see that it's true. You will discover that you *are* a great person.

I always suspected myself to be a strong person, but through certain traumatic experiences, I lost my grip on that reality. Even so, being caught up in substance abuse does not make our inner strength go away. It just makes it extremely difficult to get in touch with that strength and use it in daily life.

Drugs and alcohol are not on my path anymore. They are like run-down old shacks on the side of the road. I might look at them, but I don't visit them. I keep driving because I have more important places to go—even if I don't always know where that is.

You do not have to spend every day for the rest of your life worried about, or afraid of, alcohol or drugs. They can be like shacks on the side of the road, and you can just drive on by.

⌘

Imagine you are caught deep in a forest. All around you the dark trees and cold wind rip against your skin. There are animals screeching in the night air, and some even lash out to attack and bite you. You are trapped.

Now imagine you see a way out. You see the impression of a path carved in the foliage in front of you. Looking off in the distance, in the direction of the path, you see a dim light.

I hope what I've shared with you represents that path and that light. I hope you remind yourself often that you are important, worthy, and good, and that there is a way out of the dark forest. I hope you look for rewarding, joyful ways to support yourself. But most importantly, I hope you learn to call upon your own inner resources of strength, wisdom, beauty, and radiance.

⌘

So with great appreciation for you and compassion for any suffering that you endure as the result of substance abuse, I leave you with these five reminders:

Remember the thought, "I am doing something else now."

This is the most helpful thought that ran through my head anytime I was in a group of people who were drinking or smoking or engaging in other unhealthy behaviors I no longer wanted for myself.

It doesn't matter if you are unsure of what that "something else" is. Just know it is good and trust it will serve you in amazing ways if you continue on your path of doing something else.

Because it is nearly impossible to avoid all tempting situations all the time, you should expect to be confronted with temptation on occasion. What you can do to combat those difficult circumstances is remind yourself that you are on a different path now and it does not matter if others continue to drink— *you are doing something else now.* And it's more important to know you are *doing something else now* than it is to know exactly *what* it is you are doing. That, at times, is the fun part. You have something to look forward to, and you don't even know exactly what it is yet.

Commit to emotional growth.

Giving up alcohol and drugs is a fundamental part of recovery, but it is only *one* part. The other important part—if you want to feel better emotionally—is to be in the process of emotional transformation. This means that you *commit* to questioning your beliefs and old thought habits. It means that you pay attention to your thoughts and feelings, you explore new ways of handling them, and you make a conscious effort to find ways to nourish your spirit and soul.

That can include sitting in silent reflection, reading personal growth type books, meditation, thoughtful group discussions, one-on-one spiritual or psychological counseling, and even climbing a small mountain with a friend and working through a fear of heights. There are countless ways to explore and grow emotionally. No matter how you do it, the important thing is that you remain open to adjusting old habits of thinking that might not be serving you well.

Switch your "feeling momentum."

Many of us have spent years and years placing layer upon layer of confused, self-diminishing thoughts and feelings on ourselves. That habit creates a "momentum" of self-deprecating thoughts and feelings that is not helpful when working to overcome addictions. What is helpful is to begin the process of unveiling the true and good nature of yourself by changing the momentum of your thinking. You can do that by interrupting the self-diminishing thoughts and feelings with encouraging, *self-supportive* thoughts and feelings. You can switch from a momentum that continues to fuel feelings of self-doubt, to an uplifting momentum that continually encourages feelings of self-appreciation and love.

Nurture yourself.

You will have a much better chance of successfully giving up alcohol or drugs if you make the process as pleasant as possible. That doesn't mean it will be easy all the time. It won't. But the more good feelings you can add to the process, the more likely you will be to maintain your new habits. Things that appeal to your physical senses can be particularly helpful—things like warm showers, massages, pleasant smelling soaps, shampoos, lotions, and delicious food. Doing things that nurture your physical senses can serve as a constant reminder that *you are worthy of good things, you are worthy to be cared for,* and you are worthy of love.

It will also help to establish an exercise routine. Not only is that good for your body, but it also serves to provide you with a "place" of your own where you can go when you need a break from the stresses of life.

Eat a healthful diet. I found it really helpful to put healthy food into my body because it increased my feelings of self-worth and self-love. Make restoring your body exciting or at least interesting. Find out what you can do to strengthen, heal, and regain your physical health.

Spend time with people who share your new healthy lifestyle so you are stimulated to feel the joys of life through carefree experiences you can have with friends who are not intoxicated. They can motivate you to continue in new activities until you enjoy them naturally—or until you decide they are not for you, and you move on to explore something different.

Care for people who need it most.

Initially that means you. But even when you first quit, you can begin to think about who else might benefit from your help. I believe contributing to the well-being of others, one or many, is essential to feeling deep purpose and meaning in life, and feeling purpose and meaning is important to sustaining the desire to maintain your health and well-being.

Whether it's being kind to a stranger, helping a family member, raising money for the hungry, writing letters to the editor of your local paper, or supporting people who struggle as you have, online or in person—helping others is vital and beneficial for everyone. Allow yourself to get passionate about caring for people, and you will have a much richer and easier experience when you quit drinking or using drugs.

The main thing I want you to know is that, no matter how hopeless or trapped you might feel, you are not alone in that feeling, and you *can* get out of the forest of darkness. You can feel freer, healthier, and better overall. I have done it, and so can you.

⌘   ⌘   ⌘

"You cannot judge how well you are doing in your life based on the number of challenges that you have or do not have. However, you can assess your life on the basis of movement from earlier negative choices and experiences, to present creative, positive ones.

And, you can keep reminding yourself, 'I am the one who is doing this healing. I am the one who is learning, and growing, and choosing wisely. I am the talented, powerful, wonderful human who can keep making positive choices as long as it pleases me, day by day, throughout this lifetime.'"

Ron Scolastico, Ph.D.